Dr. Andrew V. Kudin

PHILOSOPHICAL METHODS

AND THEIR APPLICATION

TO THE ART OF LIVING

KUDIN & SONS
ACADEMIC PRESS

© 2024 Andrew V. Kudin. All rights reserved.

No part of this publication may be reproduced, stored in a retrieval system, or transmitted in any form or by any means—electronic, mechanical, photocopying, recording, or otherwise—without the prior written permission of the author, except for brief quotations or excerpts used for non-commercial educational purposes, classroom instruction, or scholarly review, provided proper attribution is given.

Published by Kudin & Sons Academic Press
California, United States
ISBN: 979-8-9989012-6-3
Printed in the United States of America

CONTENT

Introduction………………………………………..		5
PART I. Definition of a Philosophical Method……		7
PART II. Basic Philosophical Methods……………		9
Chapter 1.	Dialectical Method……………....	9
Chapter 2.	Metaphysical Method…………....	27
Chapter 3.	Hermeneutic Method…………….	44
Chapter 4.	Analytical Method…………….....	72
Chapter 5.	Deductive Method………………..	87
Chapter 6.	Empirical Method………………...	97
Chapter 7.	Phenomenological Method……….…	106
Chapter 8.	Materialist Method……………….	117
Chapter 9.	Idealist Method…………………..	125
Chapter 10.	Rationalist Method……………...	133
Chapter 11.	Critical Method…………………	142
Chapter 12.	Existential Method……………..	155
Chapter 13.	Pragmatic Method……………...	170
Chapter 14.	Historical-Philosophical Method………	183
Chapter 15.	Dialogical Method……………...	194
Chapter 16.	Deconstructivist Method…………	206
Instead of a Conclusion…………………………….		219
Literature………………………………………		221

INTRODUCTION

An artist needs a brush to paint a picture, and a gardener needs gardening tools to create a garden. Both create works of art with tools - the artist on canvas and for the gardener the canvas is wildlife - trees, shrubs, flowers...

To build a skyscraper builders need a construction crane, and a pilot needs an airplane to take passengers from one country to another.

No matter what exactly you're going to do you're going to need tools.

In the painting example, the artist is the subject, the canvas is the object, and the brush is the tool with which the subject interacts with the object to produce the desired result.

When you study branches of philosophy or philosophical categories you will also need tools. These tools are called philosophical methods.

To go further, you need a deeper understanding of what a philosophical method is and which methods you will use as your tools. In philosophy, methods are not abstractions, but practical ways of getting to the heart of things, of understanding the world and yourself. Just as a painter chooses a brush for a particular stroke, a philosopher chooses a method to analyse a particular problem. The right choice of methods determines how accurate and deep your understanding will be.

PART I
Definition of a Philosophical Method

Method in philosophy is a system of principles, rules, and procedures that aim to investigate, analyse, and comprehend various aspects of reality, knowledge, morality, being, and other fundamental issues.

A philosophical method determines the approach to posing questions and seeking answers to them, thus forming the basis of philosophical activity.

In my explanations, I will refer not only to philosophical works but also to literary works familiar to you since childhood. Reading and understanding a philosophical work requires preparation. Literary works make it easier. You relax when you read a good book and at the same time, you broaden your horizons, train your brain, get knowledge...

A talented writer is always a good psychologist. In many books, as if in mirrors, deep ideas and philosophical teachings are reflected, that is why they are so interesting to read.

PART II
Basic philosophical methods

Chapter 1. Dialectical Method

"The bud disappears when the flower blossoms, and might be said to be refuted by the flower; similarly, when the fruit appears, the flower is recognized as the false cash existence of the plant, and the fruit takes the place of the flower as its truth. These forms not only differ from each other but supersede each other as incompatible. But their fluid nature makes them at the same time moments of organic unity, in which they are not only not contradictory, but one is as necessary as the other, and it is this equal necessity alone that constitutes the life of the whole."

Georg Wilhelm Friedrich Hegel's
"Phenomenology of Spirit"

Definition:

A dialectical method is a research method that is based on the identification and resolution of contradictions through the process of dialogue or argumentation. A dialectical method considers the development of concepts and systems through the interaction of opposites, which leads to their synthesis and the emergence of new qualities.

Landmark figures:
Socrates, Plato, Georg Wilhelm Friedrich Hegel, Karl Marx.

Application:

The dialectical method is used to analyse historical and social processes, philosophical systems, and concepts.

The basic principle of dialectics is development through contradictions and their resolution. This method is used to understand complex dynamic systems in which opposites and the interaction of opposites lead to the emergence of new forms with new qualities.

The Main Components of the Dialectical Method

(a) Thesis. A thesis is the initial idea or statement with which the dialectical process begins. It can represent any idea, position, or statement that expresses a particular point of view about a situation, phenomenon, or problem. The thesis serves as a starting point for further discussion. In everyday life, a thesis can be expressed in many different forms. For example, "Summer is the most enjoyable time of the year" is a thesis that states that summer is more pleasant than other seasons. However, the dialectical process implies that a thesis is not a final truth and must be subjected to critical examination.

(b) Antithesis. Antithesis is an opposing idea or statement that arises as a reaction to a thesis. It expresses a counterargument or an opposing view that points out the weaknesses or limitations of the thesis. The antithesis helps to identify contradictions and weaknesses in the original statement. For example, the antithesis to the statement "Summer is the most pleasant time of the year" can be "But it can be unbearably hot in summer". The antithesis shows the other side of the issue and suggests that the thesis may be missing some important aspects, such as unbearably hot weather.

(c) Synthesis. A synthesis is a new idea or statement that results from the resolution of a contradiction between the thesis and antithesis. A synthesis combines elements of both statements, preserving their key ideas and resolving the contradictions. This stage leads to a deeper and more holistic understanding of the problem. For example, in synthesis, the thesis that "summer is the most pleasant time of the year" and the antithesis "but it can be unbearably hot in summer" can be combined into a new statement: "Summer is the most pleasant time of the year, which should be spent in the shade of trees or by a body of water to avoid the heat". Thus, synthesis allows the advantages of both statements to be taken into account and creates a new, more balanced understanding of the situation.

The Dialectical Method in the Context of Philosophy

The dialectical method allows us to study dynamic processes and interactions of opposites.

In the *Phenomenology of Spirit*, Hegel shows the path of development of human consciousness from the most elementary perception to the highest form - absolute knowledge. Hegel wrote that this development is not linear, but dynamic, in which each stage overcomes and simultaneously includes the previous ones. This path includes a constant encounter with limitations, contradictions, and their overcoming, which leads to a new, deeper understanding of reality. Ultimately, consciousness reaches absolute knowledge, where the subject realizes that he himself is part of the comprehensive process of being and that knowledge is not just a reflection of the world, but an active participant in its creation.

1) Sensory Perception (Thesis)

At the first stage of cognition, consciousness encounters the world through simple sensual data - what can be seen, heard, and felt by touch. Here the subject perceives the surrounding reality as a set of separate objects that exist independently of each other. This level of cognition is reminiscent of child perception: a person sees a tree, hears a bird singing, and feels the touch of the wind, but does not understand how it is all connected.

At this stage, consciousness does not yet distinguish the boundary between the inner and outer world, between the process of thinking and the external reality. It only fixes separate elements without understanding their interaction. This is a view of the world through the prism of immediate sensations, where each object is seen separately as if isolated from the others. Perception at this level is limited: it does not notice hidden connections and does not try to penetrate beyond the surface of the visible.

2) Perception (Antithesis)

At the next stage, consciousness begins to realize the limitations of mere sense perception. At this point, there appears understanding that the objects of the external world cannot be cognized solely through sensation. Consciousness is confronted with the fact that the perception of each object depends on the subject himself, on his individual senses, reason, and experience.

Here begins the first serious contradiction: a man realizes that his perception of the world is not just a reflection of objective reality, but something that passes through the prism of his subjectivity. The question becomes deeper: how is the subjective perception related to the objective world? What is the true nature of reality if it is so strongly affected by the individual's perception?

This stage raises doubts and philosophical questions: how can we distinguish the real from the illusory if our perception is inevitably subjective? We see, hear, and feel, but can we be sure that what we perceive exists exactly as we perceive it?

3) Strength and Intelligence (Synthesis)

At this stage, consciousness begins to seek ways to reconcile the contradiction between self and object, recognizing that objects do not exist in isolation, but are connected by invisible threads of forces and regularities. The subject begins to realize that the world is not a chaotic collection of individual things, but a harmonious structure where each element obeys certain laws and interacts with others.

Man realizes that behind the visible surface of things, there are forces that control their movement and change. This new understanding opens before him an ordered picture of the world, where nothing happens by chance. At this stage, however, the man still perceives these forces as something external, without directly linking them to himself. The laws of nature seem to him something independent, governing the world from the outside, and the subject does not yet realize his role in this network of interactions.

This stage is a step forward to a deeper understanding of the interconnections in the world, but for now, consciousness is still searching for an answer to the question: what is my role in this great mechanism?

4) Self-awareness

After the stage of perception and realization of contradictions between the subject and the object, consciousness reaches a new milestone - the stage of self-consciousness. At this stage, the subject does not simply observe the world but realizes himself as an active participant in the process of cognition. Man begins to realize that he does not just passively perceive reality, but also shapes it himself through his thoughts, perceptions, and actions. This turning point reveals a profound understanding that reality is not something external, detached from us, but a reflection of our inner world and our interactions with it.

However, self-awareness does not relieve contradictions. For the first time, there comes the realization that the inner world and external circumstances are in a subtle relationship. A person begins to strive for independence, for autonomy of his thoughts and actions. But at the same time, to assert his existence and significance, he needs the recognition of other people. This creates tension: how can we remain independent and integrated while recognizing that our perception of the world and ourselves is inevitably influenced by interactions with others?

Here a complex dialectic of self-consciousness opens up: a person realizes his uniqueness and independence but also understands that the fullness of this realization is impossible without interaction with others, without recognizing their presence in his world.

5) Reason

When consciousness rises to the level of self-consciousness, a new stage opens up - reason. Here man begins to explore and cognize reality through various forms of human culture: science, art, and morality. Reason strives for order, and awareness of the world through concepts, universal laws, and structures that can explain the nature of all things. It is no longer just sensory perception or subjective reflection, but an attempt to grasp and express an objective truth that lies beyond individual experience.

At this level, reason seeks to build a holistic picture of the world, in which all phenomena are subject to logic and laws. Science helps to explain material reality, art - to express deep feelings and inner experiences, and morality - to form principles that regulate relations between people. In these forms, reason seeks universal answers, trying to overcome chaos and randomness, to comprehend the laws that govern the world.

But even here there are contradictions. The gap between theoretical knowledge and practical reality becomes obvious: how can everything be explained through abstract laws, when life is full of unpredictable events and moral dilemmas cannot be solved by a single formula? This stage gives rise to new questions: can reason give us answers to all vital questions, or will there always be an area beyond its control?

Thus, reason reveals the greatness of cognition for the consciousness, but at the same time suggests new secrets and unsolved contradictions.

6) Spirit

At the stage of spirit, consciousness makes an important step from personal reason to social and cultural life. Man begins to realize himself not only as a separate individual but also as a part of society, its traditions, and cultural values. Understanding of the world acquires new depth, becoming collective.

Here a new realization is born: truth does not belong to reason alone but lives in the collective spirit, which manifests itself through accepted norms, laws, religion, and art. Each individual is but one thread in a larger fabric woven from social experience and cultural symbols. In this collective spirit, people find common meanings and values that bind them together and help them understand the world around them.

This stage leads to the realization that the world cannot be understood alone. It is through them that man finds his place in society and becomes aware of his own existence.

7) Absolute Knowledge

The final stage of cognition is the attainment of absolute knowledge, the moment when consciousness transcends all the contradictions that arose in the previous stages. Here the subject reaches the state when there is no longer a division between inner and outer, between mind and reality. The subject realizes that his own consciousness is not merely an observer but an active participant in what he is learning. Object and subject merge into a whole, and the person begins to see the world as a continuous flow of interactions, where everything is connected to everything.

At this stage, one acquires not just theoretical knowledge of reality, but an inner, deep understanding that everything that exists is a single process, continuous and integral. Absolute knowledge is a state in which the contradictions between subject and object no longer matter, they become irrelevant. Consciousness ceases to split the world into separate parts and begins to perceive it as an inseparable unity.

A person realizes that every object, every phenomenon is just a part of a huge picture of being, in which everything is interconnected and supports each other. There is no longer a division between "I" and "not I", between inner and outer - all these are just aspects of a single reality. At this stage, knowledge becomes not just cognition, but an inner experience of truth, a sense that man and the world are one and the same.

Absolute knowledge opens before the consciousness a picture of the world where every element, every event, and every action has its place and meaning in the overall harmony. It is no longer an abstract thought or theory, but a living reality, which a person can feel with his whole being.

Socrates was a master of the dialectical method, the essence of which was to question the seemingly obvious and gradually reveal the contradictions in the interlocutor's judgments. This method, known as Socratic dialogue, was not just an exchange of opinions, but a profound process of seeking truth through questions and answers. Socrates forced his students and opponents to reflect on their own beliefs so that they could see the weaknesses and inconsistencies in their own views. This was not teaching but rather a thought provocation that led to self-knowledge and awareness of incompleteness of knowledge.

Reading Plato's dialogues, it becomes evident that this method of Socrates is central to his philosophy. Plato used the dialectical approach to explore a wide variety of philosophical questions. For example, in *The Republic* dialogue, Plato explores the nature of justice through the image of Socrates. In the course of the conversation between Socrates and other participants, different opinions and points of view clash. The arguments are conducted in order to reveal not only personal views but also the deep essence of the subject under discussion.

It is through this tension of opposing ideas and arguments, through the clash of opinions that the theme is revealed. Ultimately, the discussion in *The Republic* leads to a deeper understanding of what justice is and how it manifests itself not only in an individual but also in the state. Socrates' dialectical method thus opens before the philosopher and the reader the way to the truth which is born in dialogue rather than in solitude, in constant search and research.

An example of a dialogue between Socrates and Thrasymachus:

Socrates: "Do you really think that justice is simply the benefit of the strongest, Thrasymachus?"
Thrasymachus: "Of course it is so, Socrates. Laws are made by rulers for their own benefit, and therefore justice consists in obeying those laws."
Socrates: "But may not rulers err in what is to their advantage? And if they make laws that do not benefit them, would justice then consist in following those erroneous laws?"
Thrasymachus: "You are cunning, Socrates. But even if rulers err, they remain the strongest, and therefore justice consists in obeying them."

Hegel raised the dialectical method to an entirely new level, bringing it to a high degree of abstraction and systematization. In his work *Phenomenology of Spirit*, he showed how the dialectical process underlies the development not only of individual consciousness, but also of history, nature, and reality as a whole. For Hegel, dialectics is not just a method of reasoning, as in Socrates or Plato. It is the way through which all being develops.

The essence of Hegelian dialectics is that every concept or phenomenon contains contradictions. These contradictions are inevitable because nothing exists in a static state - everything is in motion and change. But it is through the realization of these contradictions and their resolution that the transition to a new level - to a new, higher form of existence or thinking - takes place. Thus, a simple idea, when confronted with its opposite, is transformed into a more complex and perfect understanding.

For Hegel, this process of dialectical development applies to everything: human consciousness develops through conflict and resolution of contradictions, historical events, and ideas also move along this path, and even nature itself is subject to this law. In every phenomenon, its negation is hidden, but this negation does not destroy it. On the contrary, it leads to a deeper understanding of its essence.

An example from *The Phenomenology of Spirit* (section "Master and Slave"):

Hegel describes in detail the dialectical process through which consciousness passes, exploring its development at various stages. One of the key moments of this process is the interaction between master and slave, which symbolizes an important stage on the way to the formation of self-consciousness.

Hegel: "Self-consciousness achieves its satisfaction only in another self-consciousness. This achievement is a process in which two self-consciousnesses strive to recognize each other. In this struggle, one self-consciousness yields becomes a slave, and the other becomes a master. The master asserts his authority over the slave, but through this recognition, he discovers that his own freedom and independence depend on recognition by the slave, who, being in a subordinate position, cannot grant true recognition."

The master is dependent on the slave's recognition. This shows his inner contradiction: he dominates, but his dominance is not complete because he is dependent on the slave. On the other hand, the slave, while in subjugation, goes through a process of labor and transformation of nature. This leads to the development of his consciousness and understanding of his own independence. Eventually, through labor and self-knowledge, the slave achieves a higher form of self-awareness than the master.

This passage demonstrates how the contradiction between master and slave (power and subordination) is resolved in the dialectical process into a new, higher form of self-consciousness. The master loses his absoluteness, while the slave, on the contrary, through labor and awareness of his essence, develops and acquires true self-consciousness.

Hegel uses this concept to show that the development of consciousness, like the development of history and nature, occurs through dialectical movement - the process of resolving contradictions and moving to higher levels of understanding and being.

Karl Marx applied Hegel's dialectical method to the analysis of society and the economy, creating his own concept - dialectical materialism. In *Capital*, Marx uses this method to explore the contradictions of the capitalist system, primarily the conflict between labor and capital. He shows how these contradictions become the driving force of social change.

An example from the first book of *Capital*, Chapter 23, "The Universal Right of Capital Accumulation," vividly demonstrates the logic of dialectics in Karl Marx's analysis. Karl Marx writes:

"Other things being equal, as capitalist production grows, capital accumulation also develops. But the accumulation of capital means nothing more than the conversion of surplus value into capital. Thus, capital accumulates its power over labor, increasing the exploitation of the working class. This, however, leads to an increase in the size of the working class and intensification of its exploitation."

Here Karl Marx emphasizes that as capital increases, so does the exploitation of workers. Capitalists, seeking to increase profits, increase their control over labor. However, this process also leads to increasing contradictions: the greater the exploitation, the greater the workers' awareness of their situation, and the greater their desire for change.

Karl Marx continues:

"Thus, the accumulation of capital on the one hand increases the wealth of the capitalists, but on the other hand deepens the poverty, slavery, dependency, degradation, and exploitation of the working class. This inevitably leads to the situation that sooner or later a situation will arise where the working class, realizing its strength, will rise up against the capitalists to change the existing system."

These lines demonstrate how Karl Marx uses the dialectical method to analyse capitalism. The contradiction between capital and labor does not just exist; it drives the system itself. The more capitalists accumulate, the more social inequality deepens and class contradictions sharpen. Marx saw this process as the inevitable dialectic of the destruction of capitalism, since the increasing tension between labor and capital, in his view, was bound to lead either to reform or revolution.

Karl Marx sees the capitalist system as one that bears the seeds of its own destruction. The more capital seeks to accumulate profits by worsening labor conditions, the more social contradictions grow. Ultimately, these contradictions lead to the accumulation of social tensions and, as a consequence, to social explosion.

An example of the use of the dialectical method in a literary work

Goethe's *Faust*

Johann Wolfgang von Goethe used the dialectical method in his famous *Faust*. The dialectical process in this tragedy can be seen as the key basis of the plot, where the struggle of opposites and their resolution serve not only as an engine of action but also as a metaphor for the spiritual and intellectual development of the protagonist.

1) Thesis - Faust and the Pursuit of Knowledge

Dr Faust, the main character of the work, is the embodiment of the thesis - the human desire for absolute knowledge and the search for higher truths. He is a scholar who has mastered many disciplines: science, medicine, philosophy, and theology. But despite the breadth of his knowledge, Faust experiences deep frustration and inner emptiness. His quest for understanding goes beyond what is accessible to the human mind, and this unsatisfied desire pushes him further, to search for what is inaccessible through ordinary experience and logic.

Faust symbolizes mankind's thirst to comprehend the truth, which is beyond the limits of conventional understanding, the human desire to overcome the boundaries of the possible and get to the meanings hidden behind the veil of reality. Goethe through Faust reveals the unquenchable human nature, which always strives for more, to reach new heights, to understand the unknowable. Faust shows man's eternal struggle with his own limits, and his desire for higher knowledge, despite the realization of the limitations of the human mind.

Faust becomes a symbol not only of a scientist but of every human being who seeks to transcend his time and his understanding to find answers to the fundamental questions of existence.

2) Antithesis - Mephistopheles and Temptation

On the opposite side of Faust stands Mephistopheles, who embodies the antithesis. It is not just an antagonist, it is the embodiment of cynicism, doubt, and temptation. Mephistopheles is the voice of skepticism that destroys all lofty aspirations, offering his own, radically different point of view on the world. He represents the material side of existence, where there is no place for great ideals, philosophical quests, and the pursuit of truth. For him, life is a game, where pleasure and enjoyment are more important than meaning.

Mephistopheles does not simply oppose Faust's aspirations for knowledge and comprehension of higher truths. He actively proposes an alternative: to abandon the quest, not to strive for the impossible, but instead to immerse himself in the world of sensual pleasures, pleasures, and material goods. His task is to prove to Faust that his dreams of greater things are meaningless. He argues that human aspirations are futile, that all this pursuit of meaning is just an illusion, and that real life is about satisfying earthly desires.

The dialogue between Faust and Mephistopheles becomes a tense struggle of opposites. Mephistopheles is cunningly and cleverly manipulative, seeking to distract Faust from his spiritual quest and draw him into the world of carnal pleasures. Here Goethe shows the eternal conflict - man's desire for the highest is confronted with material reality, where simpler and more accessible pleasures reign.

This antithesis culminates in the bargain between Faust and Mephistopheles. Faust, frustrated in his quest and wanting to experience all the joys and possibilities of life, makes a pact with the devil. He sells his soul in exchange for receiving all that this world has to offer. For Mephistopheles, this bargain is a confirmation of his theory that in the end, every man will lean toward material things, toward momentary pleasures, rather than toward an endless and arduous search for truth.

The bargain made between them becomes not only the basis of antithesis but also demonstrates a profound philosophical clash: which is more important - higher ideals or earthly pleasures? Mephistopheles assures that man's ultimate goal is not truth but getting the most out of life, and Faust has a long way to go to realize how true this is.

3) Synthesis - New Understanding and Spiritual Transformation

However, the interaction between Faust and Mephistopheles throughout the play leads not only to destruction but also to a profound spiritual transformation of the protagonist. This dialectical process is not reduced to a simple struggle between good and evil, knowledge and sensuality - it leads to synthesis, a new understanding of life and human existence.

Faust, having gone through a series of sufferings, temptations, and the realization of his mistakes, reaches a new level of understanding. His initial desire for knowledge, which he wanted to acquire for its own sake, proves to be illusory, as do the material pleasures offered by Mephistopheles. At the end of his journey, Faust realizes that truth and happiness do not lie in superficial pleasures or in the pursuit of abstract wisdom. True perfection is hidden in spiritual development and service to others.

The contradictions that accompany him along the way - between his high ideals and the cynicism of Mephistopheles - do not destroy him, but lead him to realize the importance of harmony between the spiritual and the material. Faust realizes that man cannot exist only in the world of abstract ideas or exclusively in the material world. The true fullness of life lies in finding a balance between these two worlds.

This spiritual journey culminates in a moment of synthesis. Faust reaches the point where his quest for higher knowledge is combined with an understanding of the importance of human experience, action, and service to society. His death symbolizes spiritual rebirth rather than the end. Despite his pact with Mephistopheles, Faust is saved because his search for truth and his struggle with his own weaknesses have led him to a higher form of existence - to the realization of higher spiritual values.

The final synthesis in Goethe's *Faust* not only completes the dialectical process but also serves as a symbol of the fact that man's path to the truth is invariably full of contradictions, falls, and temptations. But even in this complex process, spiritual growth is possible, and it leads to salvation if man does not stop striving for the highest.

The dialectical method in Goethe's *Faust* is manifested through the clash of opposing forces - the desire for knowledge and skepticism, spiritual ideals, and material temptations. This conflict not only sets the movement of the plot but also reveals the inner struggle of the protagonist where each contradiction leads him to new understanding.

Faust strives for greater knowledge and understanding, but temptations constantly arise on his path, reflecting the limitations of human existence and its dependence on material things. This confrontation becomes the nucleus through which Faust gradually moves from delusion and error to a new level of realization. The dialectic here works as a process in which contradictions do not destroy one another, but lead to the development of the hero.

Goethe shows that truth is not given to man at once - it rises through constant overcoming, through struggle, and inner conflict. In this struggle, Faust discovers deeper meanings of existence. Thus, the dialectical method becomes the basis for the hero's spiritual evolution, where each new level of understanding is born out of the tension between opposites.

Goethe's *Faust* is a work in which dialectic not only structures the plot but also becomes an important philosophical tool. Goethe points out that truth is not the endpoint of the journey but is constantly renewed through movement and resolution of contradictions.

Chapter 2. Metaphysical Method

"In the universe, everything is connected and moving so that every moment of life goes away to be reborn in another place and time."
Gabriel Garcia Marquez, "One Hundred Years of Solitude"

Definition:

The metaphysical method is a method of inquiry that seeks to explore fundamental questions of being, reality, the nature of existence, and causality.
The metaphysical method seeks to understand the basic principles and structures underlying all things by looking beyond the physical world and empirical observations.

Landmark figures:
Aristotle, Immanuel Kant, Martin Heidegger.

Application:
The metaphysical method is used to analyse fundamental questions about the nature of reality, being, space and time, causality and necessity, possibility, and reality. This method is used in philosophy to develop comprehensive theories that explain the nature of all things, and in religion and theology to understand the concepts of God and spirituality.

The Main Components of the Metaphysical Method

1) Ontology.
Ontology is a branch of philosophy that focuses on studying the nature of being and existence. It attempts to

answer the fundamental questions about what it means to exist, how to distinguish the real from the illusory, what entities exist in the world, and how they interact with each other. This component of metaphysics studies material objects, and abstract concepts such as numbers and ideas, and attempts to understand the nature of consciousness and its relationship to physical reality.

One of the central themes of ontology is the distinction between essence and existence. Essence is what defines an object, what makes it what it is. Existence, on the other hand, refers to the fact of an object's presence in the world. The questions that arise in ontology are not limited to simple categories of reality; they cover the entire spectrum of being, from material things to abstract concepts and ideas, including human consciousness and its place in the world.

2) Cosmology.

In metaphysics, cosmology studies the origin, nature, and structure of the universe. It explores not just stars and planets, but deeper questions: what are time and space, how does matter come to life in this limitless cosmos, and what ultimately governs it all? Cosmology tries to look beyond the boundaries of the visible, seeking to understand how the universe came into being and whether it has a hidden meaning. Science can explain to us how galaxies evolved and how stars light up the darkness. But metaphysical cosmology goes further - it asks why it happened and what is behind it.

This section of metaphysics attempts to conceptualize the universe in its grandeur by asking questions that go beyond physics: does it all have a beginning and an end? And what does it mean for us if the end does exist? Are we merely temporary inhabitants of this cosmic scene or something more? The cosmology of metaphysics is an attempt to push the boundaries of human understanding, penetrate the mystery behind material phenomena, and conceptualize our place in this infinite space.

One of the key questions is the principle of causality: what was the root cause of this grandiose picture of existence? Was it a random explosion, or was there a deeper purpose behind it? Metaphysical cosmology plunges us into the question of whether there is a higher power that governs it all, or whether the universe evolves according to its own mysterious laws.

3) **Theology**.

Theology is a branch of metaphysics that seeks to understand the nature of God or gods, their existence, and their influence on the world. It asks questions that have preoccupied humanity since the earliest times: what is God like? Is he omnipotent, omniscient, and omnibenevolent? How does the divine will relate to the world in which we live, and what is man's place in this interaction?

Theology is not limited to abstract reflections on divine attributes. It seeks to discover exactly how God manifests himself in reality, how he interacts with humanity, and whether in this interaction there is room for a miracle or intervention from above. These questions take theology beyond the usual speculative disputes, turning it into a deeply personal reflection on the meaning of life, free will, and the moral foundations of human existence.

Theology explores various proofs for the existence of God. The cosmological argument suggests that the universe must have a first cause, which is God. The ontological argument asserts that the concept of God as a being superior to all conceivable things necessarily includes his existence. The teleological argument calls attention to order and expediency in nature, which point to a supreme design. All of this makes theology an attempt to conceptualize not only the fact of God's existence but also how his existence affects our understanding of the world.

Another important aspect of theology is the question of free will. If God is omnipotent and omniscient, how does this relate to our freedom of choice? Can a person truly be free to act if God already knows the outcome? Theology explores these subtle contradictions by reflecting on how divine will and human freedom can coexist.

Morality and ethics occupy an important place in theology because God's intervention in human life is inextricably linked to the questions of right and wrong, justice, and compassion. Theology attempts to understand how divine influence shapes moral principles and at what points in our lives this influence is most evident.

4) Essentialism.

Essentialism is a philosophical approach that seeks to understand the essence of objects and their immutable characteristics. It focuses on the question: what is it that makes an object what it is? Essentialists argue that essence precedes existence and determines the main properties of an object. It is like some kind of internal code without which the object would lose its identity.

For example, the essence of a human being, according to essentialists, may lie in the ability to think or in the fact that he or she is a rational being. These traits are not just incidental properties that can be changed without violating the integrity of the object, but something fundamental that makes a person a person.

Essentialism also distinguishes unchanging properties of an object from accidental characteristics. Accidental characteristics are those properties that can change without changing the essence of the object. For example, a person's hair color or height are accidental characteristics. They may change throughout life, but they do not change the fact that a person remains a person. However, the ability to think and to realize oneself are traits that essentialists consider unchangeable, and fundamental to the essence of a person.

Essentialism forces us to consider what lies at the heart of every object and what remains unchanged despite all the changes that occur to it over time. This view raises important questions: can essence exist independently of a material medium? And how does essence shape the very nature of an object and its place in the world?

5) The Metaphysics of Causality.

The metaphysics of causality is the study of the deep connections between events, an attempt to understand what makes one event cause another and how they are related. The questions it raises are not only about what causes things to happen but also about why events unfold in this way and not in the other. What is behind these chains of cause and effect that permeate our world?

This section of metaphysics is closely intertwined with the philosophy of time and free will, for it considers the extent to which our actions are predetermined. Are our actions conditioned by a chain of events that have already happened, or do we have true free will? If our actions are strictly deterministic, then free will comes into question. However, if there is room in the world for random events, then this opens up the possibility of true freedom.

One of the central themes of the metaphysics of causation is the distinction between necessary and accidental relations. Necessary relations imply that, under certain conditions, one event necessarily causes another. Random connections, on the other hand, occur when two events can be related, but their connection is not inevitable. This question is closely related to the broader discussion of determinism: if everything in the world is bound by necessary causes, is there any room for freedom or spontaneity at all?

In addition, the metaphysics of causality raises the question of whether it is possible for independent, non-causal events to exist. Can things that are independent of anything else happen in the world, or is everything subject to the law of causality? This opens up the prospect of a deeper understanding of how the world functions, and what role our own perception of causality plays in this.

Metaphysical Method in the Context of Philosophy

Aristotle's *Metaphysics* delves into the exploration of the nature of being, essence, and causality, forming the foundations of Western philosophy. Aristotle introduced the concept of substance - what he considered to be a basic reality that exists independently of other things. Substance for Aristotle is what makes an object itself, its essence, by virtue of which it exists.

In addition, Aristotle developed the concept of potency and act, which help explain change and movement in the world. Potency is the possibility inherent in an object, which can manifest itself but has not yet been realized. An act is the realization of that possibility, the moment when the potential becomes a reality. This distinction allows us to understand how things move from one state to another, and how development and transformation occur.

Aristotle paid great attention to the study of causes. He distinguished four causes that help explain the existence and changes of objects in the world:

1) **A material cause** is what an object is made of, its material basis.
2) **A formal cause** is the form or structure that defines what an object is.
3) **An acting cause** is the force or agent that initiates change and sets an object in motion.
4) **The ultimate cause** is the purpose or goal for which an object exists or changes.

These four causes allowed Aristotle to comprehensively explain the nature of things, their existence, and change, considering not only the physical aspects but also their meaning and purpose. Questions about the first causes and principles that underlie all things are central to Aristotelian metaphysics, making his writings one of the key works for understanding the philosophy of being.

Immanuel Kant, in *The Critique of Pure Reason*, explores the limits of human cognition and the nature of metaphysical concepts. He proposes a radical distinction between what we can know and what remains beyond our experience. Immanuel Kant introduces the concepts of "thing-in-itself" (noumenon) and "thing-for-us" (phenomenon), arguing that our knowledge is limited only to what we perceive through the senses and reason. According to Immanuel Kant, we can only cognize phenomena as they appear to us, but not the essence of things, or "thing-in-itself," which remains inaccessible to human cognition.

Immanuel Kant also takes an important step by introducing the concepts of a priori forms of sensibility - space and time. In his view, space and time do not exist independently of our consciousness, but are the forms through which we perceive the world. They are a priori, that is, given before experience, forms that structure everything we see and feel.

In addition, Immanuel Kant argues that our mind uses certain a priori categories to organize experience. These categories, such as causality, unity, and multiplicity, work like a grid through which our mind filters all impressions. Thus, even our most fundamental concepts, such as time, space, and causality, are not reflections of objective reality, but ways in which our minds structure the world around us.

Immanuel Kant emphasizes that metaphysical concepts such as freedom, the soul, or God cannot be cognized empirically because they transcend the phenomenal world. Nevertheless, these concepts are important for philosophy because they pose questions that are beyond empirical cognition but still play a key role in ethics and human thinking.

Martin Heidegger in *Being and Time* focuses on the issue of the meaning of being. He introduces the concept of "Dasein" (being-here), which denotes a unique human existence immersed in the world. For Martin Heidegger, Dasein is not just a human being as a biological being, but a being that is aware of its being and capable of asking questions about it.

One of the central themes of his work is the temporality and finitude of being. Martin Heidegger argues that human existence cannot be understood without taking time into account. Our being is always in time, and it is finite. Realizing this finitude, he argues, is a key aspect of true existence. We live in a world where the future is always directed toward the endpoint of death, and this knowledge of our mortality gives depth and meaning to our being.

Martin Heidegger distinguishes between two types of existence: authentic and non-authentic. Non-genuine existence is a life in which one evades questions about one's being, lives in vanity and superficial concerns and loses touch with oneself and the meaning of life. Genuine existence, on the contrary, implies a deep realization of one's mortality and temporality, as well as taking responsibility for one's existence.

An important aspect of Martin Heidegger's philosophy is that he does not see being as something static, but as a process that is constantly evolving. Being for Heidegger is a dynamic, changing process that cannot be fully comprehended through fixed categories. Man, being in the world, is always in motion, always in search, and it is this process of realizing his being and its finitude that determines true life.

The metaphysical method is a key tool to investigate fundamental questions of being and reality. This method allows philosophers and thinkers to go beyond the empirical world and explore the principles underlying all things.

Literary work: Gabriel Garcia Marquez's *One Hundred Years of Solitude*

One Hundred Years of Solitude is an outstanding work of magical realism, not only because the narrative interweaves miracles and other metaphysical phenomena with material reality, but also because this book broke the pattern of the materialistic realism that dominated in the late 1960s, which simply ignored all aspects of life other than the visible and tangible ones.

In *One Hundred Years of Solitude*, Gabriel Garcia Marquez explores profound questions of being, time, reality, and fate through a metaphysical method. The story of the Buendía family, covering a period of a hundred years, serves as a picturesque backdrop for reflections on fundamental aspects of human existence.

It is hardly possible to understand this work from the first time. I reread *One Hundred Years of Solitude* many times and each time I discovered this book in a new way. It was like a multifaceted "magic crystal", which, when viewed from different angles and under different lighting, highlighted different layers of reality. *One Hundred Years of Solitude* and *No One Writes to the Colonel* are associated with my student years. It was during this period of my life that I discovered Gabriel Garcia Marquez.

Major metaphysical themes in the novel *One Hundred Years of Solitude*

(a) Time and Cyclicality

In *One Hundred Years of Solitude*, Gabriel García Márquez delves into the study of time, portraying it as an endless cycle where destinies intertwine and repeat themselves like an eternal return. The life of the Buendía family is not a simple sequence of events, but a continuous cycle in which each new turn repeats the past, and history seems to close in on itself. This cyclical perception of time breaks the usual linear understanding of the past, present, and future, blurring the clear boundaries between them.

This is exemplified by the fates of the members of the Buendia family, who often repeat the fates of their ancestors. Each new generation faces the same challenges, and makes the same mistakes, as if caught in an invisible spiral from which there is no escape. Ursula, the matriarch of the family, one day notices that many events in the lives of her descendants remind her of things that have happened before as if they are reliving the fates of their ancestors. This repetitive pattern makes one wonder: do the characters have freedom of choice, or are their lives subject to the inexorable law of repetition?

Through this eternal circle of fate, Marquez asks the question of the nature of freedom: is a man truly free to control his own destiny, or are all his actions just part of an inevitable course of events that has already been predetermined? In this chaotic dance of time, the characters flounder between the hope for change and the fatal feeling that nothing will change and life is just a repetitive cycle of mistakes and loss sealed in eternity.

(b) Magical Realism and the Metaphysics of Reality

Gabriel Garcia Marquez combines the real with the magical to explore the subtle facets of reality. In the novel *One Hundred Years of Solitude*, magical events are not surprising to the characters; they become a natural part of their everyday existence. This interweaving of the fantastic and the real makes the reader think about what we consider reality and where the boundary between the real and the imaginary lies.

The scenes of Remedios the Beautiful ascending to heaven and the rain of yellow flowers that envelop the city after the death of one of the characters could serve as an example. These magical phenomena are taken for granted by the characters, with no attempt to explain them in terms of conventional logic. Magic permeates the fabric of life, dissolving the boundaries between what we would normally consider reality and what we would normally consider fantasy.

Marquez creates a world in which miracles become commonplace, thereby expanding our understanding of reality. This approach raises the question: what is actually real? Is it a reality that can be seen and touched, or does it include everything we are capable of imagining and feeling? Márquez's magical realism seems to hint that reality is multi-layered and its boundaries are only a matter of perception.

(c) Being and Essence

Questions of being and essence are central to the lives of the characters as they try to make sense of their existence and find their place in the world. In One Hundred Years of Solitude, Marquez shows how the characters strive for self-discovery while facing the limitations, the inevitability of fate, and perhaps the predetermination of their lives.

José Arcadio Buendía, the founder of Macondo, is a prime example of this struggle. His life is entirely devoted to the search for the Philosopher's Stone and the unravelling of the essence of things. He is obsessed with understanding the laws that govern the world, seeking to unlock the mysteries of nature and existence itself. His irrepressible desire for knowledge symbolizes a metaphysical desire to penetrate beyond the visible boundaries of reality, to know what lies beyond the limits of ordinary perception.

But despite his efforts, José Arcadio Buendía is confronted with the limits of human understanding and physical reality. This conflict between the desire to comprehend the essence and the realization of one's limits becomes a symbol of the struggle of every human being who tries to find answers to the most important questions: why he is here and what it means to exist.

(d) Predetermination and Free Will

One of the key philosophical issues addressed in *One Hundred Years of Solitude* is the balance between predestination and free will. The fates of the characters in the novel seem sealed in advance as if they are following a path that has already been laid out for them. However, Marquez shows that even within these predetermined destinies, the characters continue to struggle to escape the vicious circle and find their own path.

This struggle is exemplified by the people of Macondo, who often feel captive to their family name and all its recurring tragedies. They see the fates of their ancestors reflected in their own lives, as if in a spiral. However, each of them tries to change their fate, as if to prove that, despite predetermination, man is capable of choice, capable of fighting for his own future.

Marquez makes us wonder: is it possible to escape from the captivity of kin and repetitive fates? Or is this struggle just an illusion created to give the characters a sense of freedom? This theme permeates the novel, posing the eternal question - how free is man in his actions, and does he have the power to change what is destined?

Metaphysical method in the context of the work

The study of being and time

In *One Hundred Years of Solitude*, Gabriel Garcia Marquez uses a metaphysical method to explore time in-depth, presenting it as a closed circle rather than a straight line. In this circle, events do not move forward but return again and again, like an endless spiral where life repeats itself but takes on different forms in each new iteration. The Buendia family, the main focus of the narrative, lives within this closed time, facing the same life situations and tragedies across generations. This emphasizes the idea of eternal return, where each new turn of time brings its old mistakes as if imprinted on fate itself.

This cyclical nature of time in the novel makes us think about how it shapes human destinies. Time here does not just count down the days and years; it actively intervenes in the lives of the characters, influencing their decisions and destinies. Time is like a living being that dictates its rules and brings people back to the same knots of mistakes and suffering from which they cannot escape. The metaphysical method used by Marquez emphasizes that time is not just a condition of existence, but an active force that is itself a character in the novel.

The repetitive motifs and time loops in the novel symbolize not only the fatal inevitability of human suffering but also the illusory nature of attempts to escape the vicious circle of fate. This creates a philosophical question: is there freedom in human life or is everything predetermined by time and the past? The study of time in the novel goes beyond the usual linear perception, destroying the very idea of progress and change. In the context of metaphysics, time acquires an almost mythical power - it becomes both a source of torment and a profound mystery that reflects the ephemerality and illusory nature of human existence.

Magical realism as a tool for metaphysical study

Magical realism in *One Hundred Years of Solitude* becomes not just a literary device, but a means through which reality acquires new shapes. Marquez weaves magical elements with everyday scenes as if the non-existent boundary between the two worlds has long since been erased. The townspeople watch Remedios the Beautiful rise into the sky like a light cloud, and yellow flower petals floating in the air settle on the rooftops, reminding them of the fleeting nature of life. No one is surprised, no one raises their eyebrows - they live in a world where everything is possible, where miracles seem to be a natural part of existence.

The magic here is not just fantasy. Ghosts quietly enter Buendia's house, sit at tables, and talk quietly with the living, as if time has no power over them. In these scenes, Marquez creates a world where life and death are inextricably intertwined. It seems as if the shadows of the past are coming to life again, and with them come to life the questions: what is reality? And where is the boundary between existence and non-existence?

Each magical event works as a mirror in which the very nature of being is seen. The ascension of Remedios the Beautiful to heaven reflects not just a fantasy, but a longing for freedom, for going beyond the material world, for the search for something more. Magic in the hands of Márquez becomes a powerful tool with which he makes us think about what reality is and what really keeps us within its bounds.

Philosophical musings through the characters

The characters in Gabriel Garcia Marquez's novel are not just participants in the narrative; they embody different aspects of human existence, each of which is linked to deep metaphysical questions. Their lives, suffering, and death become a philosophical field in which Marquez explores the meaning of existence, the nature of freedom, and the tragedy of human destiny.

Jose Arcadio Buendia, the founder of the family, symbolizes the eternal search for truth. He strives to penetrate into the essence of things, to comprehend the laws of the world, to reveal its secrets. His unquenchable thirst for knowledge and desire to unravel the mysteries of the universe reflect the eternal human impulse to understand their place in the world. However, the deeper he plunges into this quest, the more he loses touch with reality, falling into madness. This madness is not just a loss of reason, but a metaphor for metaphysical despair in the face of infinity, in the sense of incomprehensibility of what lies beyond human comprehension. His fate asks the question: can man, in the pursuit of absolute knowledge, preserve himself, or does this attempt inevitably lead to destruction?

Colonel Aureliano Buendia, another colorful character, spends his life in endless wars. Death for him becomes something ordinary, devoid of mysticism or fear. This gives rise to philosophical reflections on free will: are his actions really a manifestation of freedom, or is he only a prisoner of his own fate, who repeats the same path over and over again, as if he were doomed in advance? Through his experience, Marquez explores the fragility of human ideals and the absurdity of war, which leaves no room for true freedom.

Amaranta, for her part, lives in anticipation of the inevitable end. Her sense of doom and her awareness of the inevitability of fate make her life seem like a long journey towards a finale, which she accepts with cold calmness. Through her, Marquez asks questions about predestination: is there an opportunity to change one's fate, or is everything predetermined? The feeling that every step leads to a known outcome creates an atmosphere of tragic acceptance and struggle with fate itself.

Each of these characters carries a piece of a large philosophical puzzle that Marquez puts together for the reader. Their fates intertwine the questions of the meaning of life, freedom, destiny, and inevitability, which make us think about what it means to be human in this world, where the answers are not always obvious, and the search often leads to despair.

Multilayered and philosophically rich

The metaphysical method that Gabriel Garcia Marquez employs in *One Hundred Years of Solitude* turns this novel into a multi-layered canvas in which every plot twist and every event is imbued with philosophical reflections on human existence. Marquez does not simply tell the story of the Buendía family; he invites the reader to reflect on fundamental questions that concern existence itself, time, reality, and death.

His approach goes far beyond the traditional narrative, turning the book into a philosophical text rich in complex ideas and profound metaphors.

Through every character, through every detail, Marquez poses to us eternal questions: what does it mean to live? What does it mean to die? What is reality and what is its essence? In his world, reality and fiction intertwine, forcing us to reconsider our usual notions of what is possible and what is not. The ascension of Remedios the Beautiful to heaven, and the silent presence of ghosts among the living - these scenes are not just elements of magical realism, they work as keys to a philosophical understanding of reality.

Marquez masterfully handles the concept of time, presenting it not as a linear sequence of events, but as a cyclical process where the past constantly returns and the future is predetermined. This philosophical exploration of time emphasizes the illusory nature of progress and asks the question: if everything repeats, can a person really change his or her destiny?

Combining magical realism with deep metaphysical reflections, Marquez creates a world in which there are no clear boundaries between life and death, real and imaginary, past and future. This approach requires that the reader should not just follow the plot, but delve into the hidden layers of the narrative, in which every event is a metaphor, every action a philosophical question.

Chapter 3. Hermeneutic Method

"Every true understanding is both a reproduction of the creative process and the establishment of the common in the context of the whole work."
Friedrich Schleiermacher's *"Hermeneutics and Criticism"*

Definition:

The hermeneutic method is a method of interpreting and understanding texts that focuses on identifying their meanings in the context of the author's culture, history, and intentions.

The hermeneutic method seeks to uncover hidden meanings and relationships that are not always immediately apparent. It offers an immersion in the text for the purpose of interpretation, paying attention to the context, cultural, and historical factors in which the text was created. This method allows us to see what is hidden between the lines and to understand the more complex ideas contained within the text, revealing the layered nature of the narrative and philosophical reflections.

Landmark figures:
Friedrich Schleiermacher, Wilhelm Dilthey, Hans-Georg Gadamer, Paul Ricoeur.

Application:
The hermeneutic method finds its application in various fields of the humanities, such as philosophy, theology, literary studies, legal studies, and cultural studies. This method is used to interpret religious texts, literary works, historical documents, and legal acts, revealing deeper meanings and

contexts. In philosophy and theology, hermeneutics helps to understand the meaning of ancient texts and teachings; in literature, it allows us to explore symbols, metaphors, and hidden layers of narrative; and in legal and historical studies, it allows us to interpret documents and laws in the context of the time in which they were created.

The Main Components of the Hermeneutic Method

(a) Text Interpretation.

Interpretation of a text is the basic process of hermeneutics, aimed at exploring its meanings and uncovering its connotations. This process goes beyond a literal understanding of the text to analyse symbols, metaphors, subtext, and even the author's intentions. Hermeneutics seeks not only to explain what a text says but also to see what is hidden behind the words, and to understand the cultural and historical context in which it was created. The interpreter penetrates beyond the obvious, realizing that the same text can give rise to many different interpretations, depending on the approach and worldview of the reader.

The main purpose of interpretation is to reveal deeper layers of the text that may not be apparent during the first reading. This includes taking into account the context in which the work was created, analysing the author's intentions, and looking for symbolic and metaphorical elements that can greatly enhance understanding of the text. This approach allows us to look at familiar works in a new way and discover hidden meanings that come to life depending on how we read and interpret the text.

(b)The Hermeneutic Circle.

The hermeneutic circle is a key principle of hermeneutics, reflecting the dynamic process of understanding a text. The essence of this method is that understanding the whole text and its parts occurs in interaction. In order to comprehend the text as a whole, it is necessary to understand its constituent elements, but these elements can only be truly comprehended in the context of the whole work. This creates a kind of circular process of interpretation: the readers immerse themselves in parts of the text, then relate them to the overall intent, and return to the details to refine their understanding.

This process is not ad hoc or linear; understanding of a text is constantly deepening, and evolving as the interpreter moves between the part and the whole. The hermeneutic circle emphasizes that understanding is never final or frozen. The reader, as if returning in a circle to the same parts of the text, finds new meanings and nuances, constantly revising his or her understanding. This principle indicates that each new look at a text can open up new horizons, allowing for deeper insights.

(c) Contextualization.

Contextualization is an important element of the hermeneutic method, involving a deep immersion in the historical, cultural, and biographical context in which the text was created. Without considering context, there is a risk of misinterpreting the key ideas and moments of work, as many meanings and implications can be lost or distorted outside of their time and setting.

For example, in order to properly understand a philosophical work, it is not enough to simply read the text; one must take into account the events of the era, the personal experiences of the author, and the cultural context in which he or she worked. Only in this way can anachronisms be avoided, where modern ideas and concepts are superimposed on the past, leading to erroneous interpretations. Contextualization helps to maintain the accuracy of the analysis and allows the reader to penetrate into the depth of the text, perceiving it through the prism of the time in which it was created.

(d) Anticipating Meanings.

The anticipation of meanings is an important aspect of hermeneutics that reflects how the interpreter enters the process of analysis with already formed expectations and assumptions about the meaning of the text. These initial hypotheses are often built on the basis of cultural, literary, or personal perceptions that guide the interpreter's first reading. However, the process of interpretation itself requires constant adjustment of these expectations. As the reader becomes immersed in the text, his or her assumptions may be refined, modified, or even completely disproved.

This aspect of hermeneutics emphasizes that no one can enter a text with a completely pure mind. We always come with a certain "baggage" of knowledge, opinions, and preconceived notions, and it is our task to recognize them, critique them, and adapt them as we delve deeper into the text. It is through this process of anticipation and adjustment that the interpreter comes closer to a more accurate and objective understanding of the meaning of the work.

(e) Dialogicality.

The dialogical nature of hermeneutics implies that text interpretation is not just a one-way process of perception, but a kind of dialogue between the author and the interpreter. The interpreter enters into an active interaction with the text, comprehending its ideas, asking questions, and rethinking initial conclusions. In this process, the text becomes not a static object, but a living interlocutor that reveals its meanings through constant interaction.

What is important is that in this "conversation," the interpreter is not a passive listener. He is actively involved in the process of interpretation, testing the author's ideas, and comparing them with his own views and the context in which the reading takes place. This interaction deepens the understanding of the work, revealing new layers of meaning that may not have been obvious in a superficial perception. Dialogicality makes the process of interpretation more dynamic and productive, turning reading into a creative act of collaboration with the author.

The Hermeneutic Method in the Context of Philosophy

Friedrich Schleiermacher is considered the founder of modern hermeneutics. He proposed a method of interpretation that changed the approach to understanding texts. Friedrich Schleiermacher developed a method that takes into account both grammatical and psychological aspects of a text, seeking to uncover not only its literal meaning but also the author's underlying intentions. For Friedrich Schleiermacher, a text does not exist in isolation from the context of its creation, so an important element of hermeneutics becomes the reconstruction of the conditions in which the author worked.

Friedrich Schleiermacher believed that the interpreter should strive to understand the author better than he understood himself, immersing himself in his world and its cultural context. This makes the hermeneutic process more than just grammatical or logical analysis: It is a deep reflection on the text as a product of human consciousness and cultural era.

Schleiermacher wrote that understanding a text required the simultaneous consideration of two levels: language (grammatical aspect) and the psychology of the author (psychological aspect). This approach allowed us to go beyond the mere analysis of words, deepening our understanding of how the author thought and what he was trying to convey.

Wilhelm Dilthey expanded the boundaries of hermeneutics by applying it to the study of historical and cultural phenomena. He argued that understanding historical events requires not only analysis of the facts but also a deep immersion in the living conditions of those who were involved. For Dilthey, interpreting history is not just studying documents or data; it is an effort to feel the experience of people who lived in a certain era, to understand their feelings and perception of the world.

Dilthey emphasized the importance of empathy - the ability of the interpreter to "live" in the world of historical figures, to feel their thoughts and emotions in order to understand how they made decisions and acted under specific conditions. This required careful analysis of not only the events but also the entire cultural milieu in which these events unfolded. Dilthey insisted that it is only through understanding the inner experience of the participants in history that one can truly grasp its meaning.

Paul Ricoeur made a significant contribution to the development of hermeneutics, especially in the field of interpretation of symbols and myths. One of Paul Ricoeur's key ideas was the concept of the "hermeneutics of suspicion", which focuses on revealing the hidden meanings behind the external content of a text. Paul Ricoeur believed that many texts, especially those associated with myths, and religious and cultural symbols, contain deep, sometimes contradictory meanings that are not always obvious at first glance.

His approach was that an interpreter should not just read the text literally, but "suspect" it by trying to uncover hidden layers of meaning. It is a method of active analysis aimed at understanding what the author may have withheld without realizing it, or what is expressed symbolically. Through symbols and myths, Ricoeur sought to show that a text can contain multiple interpretations, and the hermeneutics of suspicion helps to go beyond the explicit to reveal deeper and more complex meanings.

Hans-Georg Gadamer in *Truth and Method* develops the concept of the hermeneutic method, emphasizing that the process of understanding is always connected with historicity and dialogicality. He argues that interpretation does not take place in a vacuum - it is always embedded in the context of tradition and culture in which the interpreter finds himself. Each new reading of a text is not simply a reproduction of meaning, but an active interaction in which both past traditions and the reader's contemporary experience play a role.

Gadamer emphasizes that understanding is a never-ending process. We can never reach a final, fixed understanding of a text, for each time we return to it we bring with us new life and cultural experiences. Understanding takes the form of a dialogue in which the interpreter does not simply perceive the text but interacts with it, asking questions and discovering new meanings.

The main emphasis in Gadamer's hermeneutics is on the relationship between history, tradition, and the process of understanding. For him, understanding is always a historically conditioned process that arises at the intersection of past and present.

The Main Aspects of the Hermeneutic Method in Gadamer:

(a) The Historicity of Understanding.

Hans-Georg Gadamer emphasizes that understanding always takes place in the context of historical tradition. Every human being, regardless of his or her will, interprets the world through the prism of the cultural and historical experience that he or she inherits. Gadamer introduces the concept of preconceived notions (Vorurteile), which should not be taken as something negative. On the contrary, these preconceptions are a natural and necessary part of the process of understanding. They bind the interpreter to his cultural tradition, creating the basis for a dialogue with the text or event.

Preconceptions shape our perception of the world and help us navigate it by linking us to the cultural and historical strata in which we live. Thus, understanding cannot be completely objective and independent of the past. Gadamer argues that being aware of one's historical conditioning does not limit but rather deepens understanding, allowing us to see a text or work of art in a broader cultural context.

(b) The Dialogicality of Understanding.

For Gadamer, the process of understanding is always dialogical. This means that the interpreter and the object of interpretation - be it a text, a work of art, or a historical event - enter into a dynamic interaction where understanding is formed through exchange and active reflection. Gadamer sees this process as a kind of dialogue in which the interpreter does not simply "read" the text, but engages in a conversation with it, asking questions, seeking answers, and revising his or her position.

Gadamer introduces the concept of the hermeneutic circle to describe this process. Interpretation always begins with prior understandings or preconceived notions that the interpreter brings to this dialogue. However, through interaction with the text or object, these initial positions are refined, modified, and enriched, allowing for deeper insight into the subject matter. The process of interpretation is never complete is a constant movement where understanding is constantly evolving and renewed as the interpreter continues to interact with the subject.

For Gadamer, understanding is not a static truth, fixed once and for all. It is a living and evolving process that depends on context, time, and previous experience, but always remains open to the new.

(c) Horizon Fusion.

An important aspect of Gadamer's hermeneutic method is the concept of "horizon fusion" (Horizontverschmelzung). This term emphasizes that understanding is not just the perception of information, but a process of interaction between the interpreter and the object of interpretation. The horizon, according to Gadamer, is the totality of all the knowledge, experiences, and expectations that one brings to the process of interpretation. It is a kind of "personal frame" through which everyone perceives and conceptualizes the world.

When the interpreter encounters a text, a work of art, or a historical event, he or she interacts with another horizon - that of the subject of interpretation. In the process of dialogue, these two horizons do not remain isolated. On the contrary, they merge, whereby the interpreter goes beyond his initial understanding, broadening his view of the world. This "merging of horizons" allows the interpreter to reach a new level of understanding that is enriched by the experience of the subject of interpretation.

The merging of horizons is not a static process, but a dynamic interaction that enables the interpreter to broaden his or her perception and deepen his or her understanding. As a result, interpretation becomes not just a way of transmitting knowledge, but an active process of transformation and development, where each new contact with a text or object opens up new facets of meaning.

(d) Truth as a Process.

Gadamer argues that truth is not something static and final. In his philosophy, truth is seen as a process that never reaches full completion. Understanding, according to Gadamer, always remains open to new interpretations, revisions, and enrichments. Thus, truth is not fixed once and for all, but exists in constant motion, evolving through dialogue with tradition, culture, and other interpreters.

For Gadamer, truth is not born out of a single act of comprehension or interpretation, but in a process of interaction between past and present, between interpreter and text, and between different cultures and epochs. Understanding is always an unfinished process that allows us to discover new meanings even in familiar works. In this sense, truth for Gadamer is a living phenomenon, manifested in a continuous dialogue that goes on through generations and in each new cultural context.

An example of the use of the hermeneutic method in a literary work.

The historical detective novel ***The Name of the Rose*** (original title - *Il nome della Rosa*) by the Italian writer and philosopher **Umberto Eco**, published in 1980, is a vivid example of the application of the hermeneutic method in literature. The novel not only captivates the reader with its intricate detective intrigue but also demonstrates how important the interpretation of texts, understanding their context, and dialogue with them to reveal hidden and deep meanings. Umberto Eco, through his hero William of Baskerville, shows how the hermeneutic approach helps to unravel complex texts, symbols, and meanings, which becomes the key to understanding the truth.

The novel is set in November 1327 in a Benedictine monastery in northern Italy. The protagonist, the Franciscan monk William of Baskerville, arrives at the monastery with his young apprentice, Adson of Melk, on whose behalf the novel is narrated. William is assigned to investigate the mysterious death of one of the monks, but events take an unexpected turn as more mysterious deaths begin to occur in the monastery. William, relying on logic, knowledge, and experience, tries to uncover the cause of these crimes.

William's use of the hermeneutic method emphasizes the role of interpretation and the search for hidden meanings. He analyses not only the actions and motives of people, but also texts, symbols, and ancient knowledge that hide the key to understanding what is happening. Eco thus shows that texts and events do not speak for themselves - they need to be deciphered, to see the hidden structure behind the outer shell. And only through careful reflection, through a constant return to details and contexts can one get closer to the truth.

Major hermeneutical themes in Umberto Eco's novel *The Name of the Rose*

(a) Interpretation of Texts and Symbols.

The plot of The Name of the Rose centers on a manuscript that holds the key to solving a series of mysterious murders in the monastery. William of Baskerville, the protagonist, uses his knowledge and skill in interpreting texts and symbols to solve this complex and intricate puzzle. Interpretation for him is not just reading a text, but scrutinizing every sign, every symbol to uncover their hidden meaning and significance.

An example of his hermeneutic approach is his analysis of the monastery library, where William discovers hidden connections between the texts and the murders. He examines the manuscripts in an attempt to find patterns and symbolic indications that might shed light on the tragedies taking place. His attention to the smallest details, to symbols, and hidden hints becomes a key element of the investigation. Through his ability to penetrate beyond the outer layer of the text and discover underlying connections within it, William moves toward solving the mystery.

This work with texts and symbols is a prime example of the hermeneutic method, which demonstrates that understanding and truth require constant dialogue with the text, careful reflection, and interpretation, especially when answers are hidden behind symbols and allegories.

(b) The Hermeneutic Circle.

The process of understanding in The Name of the Rose perfectly illustrates the concept of the hermeneutic circle, where understanding the whole text always depends on understanding its parts, and vice versa. William of Baskerville does not simply gather facts; he constantly rethinks and adjusts his interpretations, returning to the data he has already studied and discovering new meanings in it based on new knowledge and context. This constant movement between the part and the whole helps him to deepen his understanding of what is happening and advance his investigation.

An example of the hermeneutic circle is his method of working with books and manuscripts. William repeatedly returns to the same texts he has already studied, each time discovering new layers of meanings and hidden connections. He gradually realizes that the original interpretations were incomplete, and new data, contexts, or events illuminate them from a different perspective. This process of constant revision and deepening of his analysis helps him move toward solving the mystery of the monastery murders.

The hermeneutic circle in the novel emphasizes that understanding requires a constant dialogue between text and interpreter, as well as the ability to return to what is already known with a new understanding, discovering newer and newer layers of meaning.

(c) Contextualization.

William of Baskerville realizes that in order to interpret texts correctly, one must take into account the historical and cultural context in which they were created. He realizes that texts, especially manuscripts from the monastery library, cannot be properly understood without knowledge of the philosophical and religious debates relevant to their time. Contextualization becomes an important element of his method, allowing him to penetrate deeper into the meaning of the texts.

An example of this approach is William's study of the religious and philosophical debates of his time. He analyses the impact of heresies, dogmatic conflicts, and the political intrigues of the church on the behavior of monks and the ulterior motives behind their actions. William realizes that the books he examines were written in a context where philosophical ideas and religious beliefs played an important role, and without taking into account this cultural background it is impossible to uncover their true meaning.

William uses contextualization as a key element of his work, understanding that a text always reflects the era in which it was created. Without making sense of this context, interpretation will remain superficial and fail to reveal the underlying connections hidden in the text.

(d) Dialogicality.

In The Name of the Rose, the understanding of the text is presented as a dialogical process between the author and the interpreter. William of Baskerville, examining the manuscripts of the monastery library, seems to dialogue with their authors, trying to penetrate their thoughts, intentions, and motives. This process of comprehension turns into an active interaction with the texts, where William does not just read, but "talks" with their creators, trying to unravel their intentions.

An example of this dialogicality is William's communication with his student Adso. William not only shares his hypotheses and findings but also discusses them with Adso, who helps him refine or even revise his interpretations. This dialogue between the two not only helps to verify theories but also allows William to see things from a different perspective and open up new interpretive possibilities. Through his discussions with Adso, William deepens his understanding of the texts, confronting new questions that lead to a fuller discovery of the truth.

Dialogicality emphasizes that understanding is never isolated. It always develops through interaction, whether with the text, the author, or other participants in the process of interpretation.

The Hermeneutical Method in the Context of the Novel *The Name of the Rose*

(a) Interpretation of Manuscripts and Symbols

Manuscripts and books as sources of knowledge.
In *The Name of the Rose*, manuscripts, and books act not only as sources of knowledge but also as dangerous repositories of secrets that can lead to tragic consequences. The library of the monastery is a symbol of the control of knowledge, a place where access to certain texts is strictly limited and some of them contain heretical or threatening ideas. Books become subjects that require hermeneutic analysis because their contents are not always obvious and sometimes contain dangerous truths that can be devastating.

William of Baskerville applies the hermeneutic method to get to the heart of these complex and mysterious manuscripts. He realizes that each text is not just a record, but a coded message that needs to be deciphered. His approach is based on the fact that behind the visible content lie deep meanings that can only be interpreted through a close examination of context, authorial intentions, and historical circumstances. William carefully analyses these texts, as if to "uncover" their inner layers of meaning.

An example is his work with manuscripts containing dangerous or heretical ideas. He does not just read them, but analyses them in detail, as if he were deciphering hidden messages that might have gone unnoticed on a superficial level. His ability to see beyond the text to the hidden intentions of the authors helps him advance his investigation by revealing non-obvious connections between the texts and the tragic events at the monastery.

William's hermeneutical approach helps not only to understand the text on its literal level but also to penetrate its hidden meanings, which allows him to uncover secrets guarded for centuries.

Symbols and signs as clues.

The Name of the Rose is saturated with symbols and signs that play a crucial role in unraveling the mystery and moving the plot along. William of Baskerville, as a philosopher and scientist, uses the hermeneutic method to analyse these symbols, trying to understand their meanings and make connections to the events that take place. Each symbol in the novel becomes not just an element of the plot, but part of a deeper mystery that requires careful interpretation.

For example, the Latin phrases scattered throughout the texts and the symbols carved on the bodies of the victims cannot be understood without their context. William realizes that these symbols carry hidden messages that require comprehension in the context of cultural and historical features. The architectural elements of the monastery also become part of this complex symbolic world: the labyrinth of the library, the geometric patterns, and the arrangement of the rooms all conceal deep meanings that help to unravel the mystery.

William realizes that the meaning of symbols and signs cannot be isolated; it always depends on the context in which they appear and the time and place in which they were created. His ability to see the connections between symbols and events allows him to move forward in his investigation, unraveling mysteries that seemed unsolvable. He reveals that behind each symbol is a complex historical and philosophical layer that must be considered in order to comprehend their full meaning.

The hermeneutic analysis of symbols in the novel not only helps William to understand what is happening but also emphasizes the importance of a contextual approach. Only through meaningful analysis and a deep understanding of all the elements of the plot can one arrive at the true solution to the mystery.

The Hermeneutic Circle.

William of Baskerville uses the concept of the hermeneutic circle to solve the complex problem of investigation. Understanding the whole - the plot and chain of crimes - is inextricably linked to understanding its individual parts - texts, characters, and details. Each new step in the investigation forces Wilhelm to return to the facts he already knows, revising them in the light of new data. This process of rethinking and interpretation becomes a key element of the hermeneutic method, which helps Wilhelm to go deeper into the essence of what is happening and get closer to the truth.

By applying the hermeneutic circle, William constantly refines his interpretations, reinterpreting the meanings of symbols and texts as new information becomes available. This method allows him to see the relationship between seemingly unrelated facts and details. As an experienced philosopher, he realizes that each new discovery can change the big picture, and by returning to the data he has already studied, he finds new meanings and subtexts in them.

William's process of interpretation is continuous, and each new step in the investigation requires not only the analysis of new data but also the revision of old data. This constant movement between the part and the whole allows him and his apprentice Adson to gradually uncover hidden connections that had eluded first consideration. The hermeneutic method in the novel emphasizes that understanding is never static - it always requires development and a new look at known facts.

(b) Historical and Cultural Context.

The historical and cultural context in the novel *The Name of the Rose* plays a key role not only in creating an authentic medieval atmosphere but also in developing an in-depth understanding of the characters' motives and the meanings of the texts and symbols that William of Baskerville encounters. Umberto Eco, as a connoisseur of medieval philosophy and theology, utilizes a rich historical and cultural background to show how deeply context can influence the interpretation of events, texts, and the very ideas that permeate the novel. This allows the reader to better understand the era and the complex processes that take place in the monastery, and to realize how the past shapes the present through traditions, fears, and prejudices.

Medieval monastery as a microcosm of the epoch.

The novel is set within the walls of a Benedictine monastery in 1327, against the backdrop of the sweeping changes that were taking place in Europe. Eco depicts the monastery as a closed system, a microcosm where the religious, intellectual, and political forces of the time are concentrated and intertwined. Wilhelm and his student Adso find themselves in this world, which is a kind of model of medieval Europe, where knowledge, philosophy, and theology are under the control of the church. In this monastery, as in Europe as a whole, philosophy, and religion play key roles in shaping people's worldviews, determining which ideas can be considered safe and which are dangerous or heretical.

The monastery becomes an ideal illustration of a medieval culture that seeks to preserve tradition and protect society from new, potentially destructive ideas. Knowledge here is concentrated in libraries, but access to this knowledge is strictly controlled, emphasizing the importance of cultural and religious context in the interpretation of texts and ideas. Eco masterfully shows how the cultural biases of the time influence the behavior of the monks, their fear of heretical ideas, and their desire to suppress anything that threatens the established order.

Theological and philosophical debates.

Against the background of the complex intellectual and theological debates of the time, the novel raises questions that were relevant to medieval philosophy and theology. Among these questions are the nature of evil, free will, and the role of knowledge and laughter in human life. William of Baskerville finds himself at the center of these debates, confronting the various religious and philosophical views that shape the intellectual climate of the monastery.

One of the key issues discussed in the novel is the permissibility of laughter in religious life, which is related to Aristotle's book on comedy, which is the subject of the plot. The debate about the role of laughter reflects the tension between strict religious asceticism and the more open approach to knowledge and human nature that William preaches. Philosophical reflections on the nature of laughter become a metaphor for the broad struggle for freedom of thought and the right to question dogma. William, representing a rational approach to knowledge, faces opposition in the form of monks seeking to maintain the status quo and suppress dangerous ideas that threaten ecclesiastical authority.

Political and religious conflicts.

The novel is set during a period of intense political and religious conflicts, such as the struggle between the papacy and the emperor, as well as internal disputes between various monastic orders. These conflicts do not simply serve as a backdrop to events but have a direct impact on the behavior of the characters and the development of the plot. William of Baskerville, as a Franciscan friar, represents an order critical of the papacy, and this is directly reflected in his attitude towards the power of the monastery and his perception of what is happening.

These political and religious conflicts have a great influence on the behavior of monks and their attitudes toward forbidden knowledge. The desire to hide certain books in the monastery may be due to the fear that these texts would undermine the authority of the church and awaken heretical ideas among the monks. William, aware of these political and religious forces, uses them as a key to understanding why certain ideas and books are considered so dangerous. Eco masterfully weaves these conflicts into the overall plot, showing how politics and religion interact and influence the course of history.

The role of tradition and authority.

In medieval culture, authority and tradition played a central role, and this is reflected in the life of the monastery, where characters treat books as sources of truth, but at the same time fear their power to destroy the familiar world. Texts in the novel become symbols of both knowledge and power. They can be a source of both truth and heresy, and this duality makes the monks see books as both sacred and dangerous.

William of Baskerville realizes that every era, including his own, interprets the past through the lens of its preconceived opinions and cultural needs. He recognizes that the monks' fears of new ideas stem from their desire to maintain the status quo and avoid radical change. This historical and cultural context helps William understand why the crimes in the monastery are linked to attempts to control knowledge. Those who seek to maintain power are willing to commit crimes to suppress dangerous ideas that might undermine their position.

Eco uses historical and cultural context to create a deep and multi-layered novel in which every element, from philosophical debates to political intrigue, becomes part of a complex system that reflects the reality of medieval Europe.

(c) The Hermeneutic Circle Process.

The process of the hermeneutic circle in The Name of the Rose is illustrated through the steps that William of Baskerville takes in his investigation as he encounters enigmatic texts, symbols, and events that require complex interpretation.

Initial interpretation.

William begins his investigation with a preliminary understanding of the situation based on his experience, knowledge, and observations that he makes when he first comes into contact with the environment of the monastery. He encounters mysterious signs and texts in the monastery's library, as well as obscure symbols that are encountered during his investigation. At this stage, his understanding of the events is limited by the data he received in the early stages of the investigation, as well as his own preconceptions and expectations that he brings with him based on previous experiences. This is the initial stage of the hermeneutic circle - the moment when interpretation is still raw, based on fragmentary information.

Obtaining new data and revision.

However, once William receives new data-whether it is the discovery of previously unknown texts, new symbols, or details of a crime-he returns to the elements he has already read and analysed and revises his initial conclusions. This process of interaction between new data and previous knowledge is a central part of the hermeneutic circle. Each new piece of information changes the context of understanding, forcing William to revise his initial hypotheses.

An example would be when William finds a new text or uncovers a new symbol that changes his initial assumptions about the criminals' motives. For example, the discovery of new evidence or the parsing of Latin phrases may shed light on how the criminals' schemes work, requiring a revision of previous conclusions. This constant process of revision shows that each new discovery requires rethinking and reinterpreting what is already known.

Mutual complementation of parts and whole.

The hermeneutic circle is based on the complementarity of the parts and the whole. William realizes that each part of the investigation, whether it is a text, a symbol, or even a small detail, has meaning only in the context of the whole picture of events. However, in order to get closer to the truth, he needs to carefully analyse each part. In this process, each new discovery contributes to the understanding of the big picture, which in turn helps to uncover the significance of the individual elements.

For example, Latin phrases or symbols found in the monastery may seem disparate and meaningless in the initial stages of the investigation. However, as William connects these elements to the overall background of the events taking place, they begin to form a coherent picture. These phrases or signs find their place in the larger interpretation and provide clues to the clues. In this way, William combines the various fragments into a coherent whole as he progresses, gradually coming closer to a final understanding.

Gradual deepening of understanding.
The hermeneutic circle process emphasizes that understanding is not fixed and final. It is always in a state of development. William realizes that each new discovery, whether of a text or symbol, requires a reinterpretation of previous findings, making his understanding ever deeper and more precise. However, even as the investigation moves forward, the process is never fully complete, as each new element can radically alter the understanding of the big picture.

This hermeneutic process in the novel emphasizes that the search for truth is a continuous movement, where each new piece of knowledge not only reveals the past but also provides new directions for future reflection. William continues to deepen his understanding, realizing that each fragment he finds is another detail that gradually adds up to a picture, but always leaves room for new discoveries.

(d) Dialogic.
Dialogicality is a key aspect of the hermeneutic method, which Umberto Eco demonstrates through the figure of William of Baskerville. William not only reads and interprets texts, but he actively dialogues with their authors, trying to penetrate the essence of their intentions and understand the philosophical and religious contexts in which they were created. This dialogue becomes a kind of mental engagement with past eras and ideas.

In addition, William is in constant dialogue with his student Adson of Melk. By discussing his ideas, hypotheses, and findings with Adso, he tests his interpretations, rethinks them, and refines them. Adso plays an important role in this process: through his questions and reflections, Wilhelm is able to analyse in greater depth the texts and events they encounter. This interaction between mentor and student enriches them both, as the dialogue allows William not only to explain his thoughts but also to seek new answers.

Dialogicality in the novel reflects the very essence of the hermeneutic method, where truth is not perceived as something fixed. It is born and developed through active interaction with texts, ideas, and people. Through this process, William is able to uncover hidden layers of meaning and come closer to unraveling the mysteries of the monastery.

(d/1) Dialogue with texts and their authors.

Interpretation as dialogue.
For William of Baskerville, the process of reading and analysing a text is not a passive perception of information, but an active participation in a dialogue with its author. William sees the text not as something static, but as a living discussion in which he must engage in order to truly understand the meanings embedded in it. This process requires not just close reading, but constant questioning of the text: what exactly did the author want to express? In what context was this text created? What hidden meanings or intentions might lie behind the words? This immersion in dialogue allows William to go beyond superficial understanding and find deeper layers of meaning.

The method of hermeneutic dialogue is vividly demonstrated when William encounters the Latin texts found in the monastery. He does not simply read them word for word but seeks to penetrate hidden layers of meaning that may have been lost or misunderstood. William analyses each word to understand the author's intentions and how they relate to current events at the monastery. He uses his knowledge and experience to 'walk the talk' with the text, reconstructing the context in which it was produced and relating this to the philosophical and religious debates of the era.

Talking to tradition.

William dialogues not only with specific texts but also with the broad intellectual and cultural tradition that these texts embody. Each text with which he works is not an isolated artifact, but part of a centuries-old discussion of religious, philosophical, and ethical issues. William realizes that interpretation requires inclusion in this larger context, which includes traditions, attitudes, and ideas that have been shaped over the centuries.

For example, his discussions with Adson concern not only Aristotle's specific text on laughter but the entire tradition of religious debate about the role of laughter in human life. This text becomes part of a larger cultural dialogue that has been going on for centuries, and William engages in this dialogue through his interpretation. He tries to understand how traditional views and innovative ideas relate to each other and how they influence the events taking place in the monastery. The dialogue with text and tradition allows him to gain a deeper understanding of the philosophical and religious conflicts surrounding him and to come closer to solving the mysteries.

(d/2) Dialogue with Adson.

The student as a dialogue partner.
Adson of Melk plays a key role in the hermeneutic process, acting not just as an observer but as an active participant in the dialogue with William. Despite his youth and inexperience, Adson is an important partner in the discussion of ideas and in the search for truth. Wilhelm often shares his reflections, hypotheses, and doubts with him, and their dialogue becomes an integral part of the interpretation process. Adson asks questions that may seem naïve at first glance, but they encourage Wilhelm to revise his conclusions, find new meanings, and deepen his understanding of the text or events.

The dialogues between William and Adson illustrate that understanding is formed not only through personal reflection but also through interaction with another person. These dialogues help both participants uncover hidden meanings and gradually make progress in understanding complex issues.

Through these discussions, William does not simply impart knowledge to his student but actively participates in their joint search for truth. Dialogue becomes a mechanism through which both participants are enriched with new ideas and better understanding.

Mutual learning.

The dialogues between William and Adson also demonstrate the concept of mutual learning. Although William, as a mentor, has more experience and knowledge, he himself learns from Adson. Adson's questions and his views on ethics, morality, and the philosophy of laughter encourage William to reconsider his positions and seek more accurate and deeper answers. This process of interaction shows that dialogue is not a one-way transfer of knowledge from mentor to student, but a complex interaction in which both parties can enrich each other.

For example, in their discussions about the role of laughter in religious life, Adson does not simply listen to William's explanations, but actively participates in the reflection by asking questions that cause William to reconsider his views on the subject. Through this dialogue, William not only educates Adson but also deepens his own understanding of these issues, which demonstrates the importance of searching for truth together. This process allows both to not only better understand the texts, but also to reexamine their beliefs and philosophical views, making the dialogue a true tool of the hermeneutic method.

(d/3) Dialogue as a method of uncovering hidden meanings.

Dialogicality in The Name of the Rose emphasizes the importance of active interaction for a full understanding of a text or situation. William of Baskerville, by engaging in dialogue with the texts, their authors, and his student Adson, deepens his interpretations by uncovering meanings that remain hidden in a superficial reading. This dialogic process, which is at the heart of the hermeneutic method, helps him unravel the complex, multi-layered mysteries of the novel and come closer to the truth.

Dialogue with the text allows William to go beyond a literal reading, forcing him to think about the hidden motives, historical contexts, and philosophical ideas embedded by the authors. The interaction with Adson enriches this process, as the student's questions help William revise his hypotheses and reflections. This demonstrates that understanding is not possible without active participation and mutual exchange of ideas.

Umberto Eco shows through his novel that hermeneutics is not just an analytical method, but a way of thinking that requires openness to new interpretations and a constant dialogue with the source of knowledge. This approach helps not only to solve mysteries but also to gain a deeper understanding of cultural, religious, and philosophical contexts.

The hermeneutic method becomes a powerful tool for interpreting texts because it allows us to uncover deep and hidden meanings that are not immediately apparent. This method is important not only for philosophy but also for literature, theology, and other humanities because it contributes to a deeper and more multilayered understanding of texts and cultural phenomena.

Chapter 4. Analytical Method

"Meaning and significance are two aspects of the same expression: one tells us what the expression signifies, the other how it does it."
Gottlob Frege's "On Meaning and Significance"

Definition:

The analytical method is an approach that focuses on logical and linguistic analysis to achieve clarity and precision in concepts and expressions. This method involves breaking down complex problems into simpler components and examining them in detail.

Landmark figures:
Bertrand Russell, Ludwig Wittgenstein, Gottlob Frege.

Application:
The analytical method is used to analyse linguistic expressions in-depth, decompose logical structures, and disassemble philosophical arguments into their individual elements. This method does not just help to deal with the surface layers of meaning, it allows us to explore the essence of concepts and reveal hidden connections between them.

Applying the analytical method helps to clarify the meaning of complex concepts, avoiding ambiguity or inappropriate generalizations. For example, when philosophers discuss fundamental categories such as "freedom" or "justice," the analytical approach helps to break these concepts down into simpler components, examine each aspect separately, and propose more precise definitions. In this process, it is possible to reveal not only what is hidden in explicit terms, but also what remains unspoken or implicit.

The analytical method is also important for structuring and testing arguments. By breaking them down into logical steps, it is possible to clearly see where mistakes have been made or where the logic becomes flawed. This method helps to identify logical fallacies such as incorrect conclusions or hidden premises, which is especially important in debates where truth becomes the subject of argument. The analytical method promotes a more coherent system of knowledge, enabling one to expose weaknesses in arguments rather than simply constructing them.

In philosophy, where every detail is important, this method helps not only in the development of theory but also in the ability to formulate one's thoughts clearly and accurately.

The Main Components of The Analytical Method

(a) Decomposition means breaking down complex problems, concepts, or ideas into simpler and more comprehensible elements in order to make them the subject of deep and comprehensive analysis. In philosophy, where complex categories are often associated with abstract concepts, such decomposition helps to reveal the fundamental aspects of each problem.

For example, when a philosopher is confronted with the concept of happiness, he or she can start by decomposing this concept into its components: satisfaction of physical needs, emotional state, moral satisfaction, and social conditions. By examining each component separately, it becomes easier not only to understand the essence of the concept itself but also to realize how various factors influence the overall picture.

This approach avoids superficial consideration and allows us to see the true mechanisms behind complex phenomena. Dividing it into components creates a basis for further analysis, making problem-solving more accessible and systematic.

(b) Logical analysis involves the application of formal logic to the study and evaluation of philosophical arguments. Logical analysis helps not only to understand the structure of an argument but also to understand the validity of the conclusions drawn. It helps the philosopher to examine whether the conclusions are logically correct, whether they follow from the proposed premises, and whether there are hidden logical errors in the chain of reasoning.

Logical analysis allows us to apply such tools as syllogisms, deduction, and induction. For example, a syllogism can be used to check the correctness of the construction of simple arguments, where the conclusions follow strictly from two premises. If one of the premises is incorrect or contradictory, the entire conclusion loses validity. Logical deduction helps to investigate arguments arising from general principles, while induction allows us to draw conclusions on the basis of particular cases, gradually generalizing them.

Logical analysis makes it possible not only to evaluate the truth or falsity of statements, but also to identify subtle logical errors, such as false premises, erroneous conclusions, or lack of connection between arguments. As a result, logical analysis becomes an important tool for constructing more accurate and consistent arguments, avoiding the fallacies and confusion that can arise when a text or theory is not examined closely enough.

(c) Language analysis. Language is at the heart of philosophical research, for it is through language that ideas, concepts, and arguments are expressed. However, language is not always clear and precise and is therefore often a source of ambiguity and misunderstanding. Linguistic analysis is an important component of the analytical method, which aims to investigate linguistic expressions and their meanings in order to eliminate such problems.

This approach involves scrutinizing how words and phrases are used in philosophical texts in order to clarify meanings and eliminate possible misinterpretations. Analysts strive to ensure that each term is unambiguous and understandable because, without a clear definition of concepts, it is impossible to construct a convincing argument or conduct an in-depth philosophical analysis.

For example, concepts such as "freedom", "justice" or "truth" can be interpreted differently depending on the context. Language analysis helps to identify these differences and offers more precise definitions to avoid confusion. Such a method is also used to check that terms are used correctly so that there are no logical or semantic errors. Clear language is the foundation of clear thought. Eliminating ambiguity helps to better understand philosophical ideas and make them more accessible for analysis and discussion.

(d) Clarification of concepts. One of the key challenges for philosophy is to achieve clarity and precision in the use of concepts, as common terms can often have multiple interpretations, causing confusion and misunderstanding. Clarifying concepts becomes an important step towards a deeper understanding of philosophical questions and issues. This process involves carefully defining the meanings of concepts, investigating their context, and finding the best way to use them within philosophical discourse.

Philosophical concepts such as "being", "freedom", "consciousness" or "justice" often remain vague unless clearly demarcated. Different schools of thought may give them different meanings, leading to divergent interpretations of the same issues. Clarification of concepts helps to bring disparate meanings to a common understanding, thus avoiding ambiguity and facilitating more accurate communication of ideas.

The process of clarifying concepts is closely related to linguistic analysis since philosophical ideas are expressed through language. Philosophers strive to make its use as precise as possible so that each word reflects a clear and justified thought. The elimination of ambiguities in the use of concepts helps to avoid superficial and unclear reasoning, which, in turn, improves the quality of argumentation and contributes to a deeper exploration of the topics under discussion.

Clarification of concepts leads to the creation of a precise language of philosophy on which logical and coherent reasoning can be built. This is an essential component of the analytic method, for without a clear understanding of what we are discussing, it is impossible to achieve true knowledge or to construct a sound philosophical theory.

(e) Verification and falsification. This component of the analytical method focuses on verifying the truth of statements through logical analysis and consistency with evidence. Verification is the process of confirming hypotheses and theories by testing whether statements are consistent with observed facts or known scientific data. This approach provides assurance that conclusions are not arbitrary but are supported by objective evidence.

Falsification, in turn, has the opposite function. It tests whether claims can be disproved in the presence of contradictory data or new facts. Philosophy and science develop through criticizing and testing established theories: if a statement cannot be falsified, it becomes less credible because its limitations cannot be understood. For philosophy, this is particularly important because ideas and hypotheses must not only be logically consistent but also able to withstand criticism in the light of new discoveries or contrary data.

Verification and falsification work in tandem to help separate true claims from false ones and make philosophical reasoning more reliable and valid.

The Analytical Method in the Context of Philosophy

Bertrand Russell is one of the founders of analytic philosophy. In *The Problems of Philosophy*, Bertrand Russell applies logical and linguistic analysis to the detailed treatment of major philosophical problems. His approach is to strive for maximum clarity and precision in definitions and argumentation, which is the basis of the analytic method.

Bertrand Russell, like other analysts, believed that many philosophical disputes arise from confusion of terms and imprecise concepts. He made extensive use of logical analysis to identify internal contradictions and implicit premises in arguments. The logical rigor sought by Bertrand Russell allowed him to shatter many traditional philosophical illusions by presenting philosophy as a discipline based on clear and verifiable statements.

In addition, his use of linguistic analysis helped to eliminate the ambiguities that often lurked behind the surface meanings of philosophical expressions. Bertrand Russell showed that a significant part of philosophical problems can be solved or reformulated if the concepts used are properly analysed.

Ludwig Wittgenstein applied the analytical method in his early work *Tractatus Logico-Philosophicus* to investigate the relationship between the logical structure of language and reality. Wittgenstein argued that a large part of philosophical problems arises from the misuse of language and the misunderstandings that arise when trying to express complex thoughts in imprecise or unclear language.

He insisted that in order to eliminate these problems, language itself must be carefully analysed. In his view, every sentence must accurately reflect reality, and philosophical disputes often stem from the fact that language ceases to be an instrument of clear expression and becomes misleading. Wittgenstein believed that if one analysed the structure of sentences, revealing their true logical meaning, many philosophical problems would simply disappear, being mere illusions generated by linguistic confusion.

Gottlob Frege made a significant contribution to the development of logic and analytic philosophy, becoming one of the founders of modern logical semantics and the theory of meaning. His work laid the foundation for the subsequent development of the analytic method, which was actively used by philosophers of the 20th century. Gottlob Frege used formal logic to analyse both mathematical and philosophical concepts, offering clear and rigorous methods for investigating truth.

One of his key achievements was creation of a system in which it was possible to distinguish between sense and meaning (Sinn and Bedeutung), which made it possible to determine more precisely how different expressions in language relate to reality and the conceptual world. Gottlob Frege showed that analysing language and its logical structure was an important tool for philosophy, especially in resolving questions related to mathematics and conceptual analysis. His

methods made it possible to accurately distinguish and investigate the nature of statements, a milestone in the development of analytic philosophy.

Gottlob Frege's work on formal logic had an enormous influence on philosophers such as Bertrand Russell and Ludwig Wittgenstein and became the basis for philosophical studies of language and logic for many years to come.

When it comes to detectives, the first name that comes to mind is **Arthur Conan Doyle**. His legendary hero, Sherlock Holmes, skillfully applied analytical, deductive, and empirical methods in his investigations. Arthur Conan Doyle created the image of a detective who solves the most difficult problems, relying on logic, observation, and strict adherence to the facts.

The Analytical Method in The Practice of Sherlock Holmes.

Sherlock Holmes paid special attention to all facts and details, basing his conclusions on logical analysis and deduction. His method was to break down complex problems into their constituent elements, allowing him to scrutinize every detail and thus gain a complete picture of events. Every little thing mattered, whether it was the clothing or behavior of a person, and Holmes was masterfully able to connect them into a single logical picture.

Example 1. In Arthur Conan Doyle's story *A Scandal in Bohemia*, Sherlock Holmes demonstrates the art of analysing human behaviour. He scrutinizes the appearance and manners of his visitors to determine their origins, intentions, and even social standing. Holmes pays attention to clothing, manner of speech, accents, and style of behavior to draw accurate conclusions about each person. This keen observation and logical thinking allow him to quickly and accurately uncover people's motives, which aids him in his investigations.

Example 2. In Arthur Conan Doyle's story *The Purple Ribbon*, Sherlock Holmes uses the analytical method with remarkable precision. He focuses on seemingly insignificant details: the sound heard at night and the position of the furniture in the room. These seemingly disparate elements become for Sherlock Holmes the key to solving the mystery. By breaking down the observations into their components, Sherlock Holmes analyses every aspect, from the acoustic features of the room to the possible reasons for moving the furniture. Through this careful parsing of details, he links them into a logical chain that leads him to the correct conclusions and solving of the crime.

Example 3. In the novel *The Hound of the Baskervilles*, Sherlock Holmes once again demonstrates his remarkable ability for detailed analysis by scrutinizing every piece of evidence. He carefully analyses footprints on the ground, cryptic messages, and other evidence to connect them to the chain of events taking place. Step by step Sherlock Holmes eliminates false theories and hypotheses that would confuse a less careful investigator. His analytical method allows him to get to the heart of the matter and discover the true cause of the mysterious events, despite all the mystical hints surrounding the story.

Sherlock Holmes uses the analytical method to break down complex cases into individual facts and clues, linking them into a logical chain that leads to plausible explanations. His methodology is based on consistent and accurate analysis of every detail, which allows him to get to the heart of the case and solve even the most intricate mysteries. Here are the main stages of the Sherlock Holmes methodology:

(a) Observation. Sherlock Holmes pays exceptional attention to observation. He scrutinizes every detail at a crime scene, including those that may seem unimportant at first glance. For him, every little detail can be a clue, whether it is a fingerprint, the position of objects, or even a random sound.

(b) Data Interpretation. Based on the observations collected, Sherlock Holmes uses his knowledge, experience, and intuition to interpret the data. He looks at each detail not in isolation but in context, comparing it with other clues and events. This step allows him to identify connections between disparate facts.

(c) Formulation of Hypotheses. After interpreting the data, Sherlock Holmes formulates hypotheses based on the observations and their logical analysis. He creates several possible explanations, testing them for internal consistency and probability.

(d) Hypothesis Testing. Sherlock Holmes does not just rely on theoretical conclusions - he tests his hypotheses through further observations and experiments. This stage is the key to confirming or disproving hypotheses. By doing so, Holmes eliminates false theories and finds the true explanation of events based on facts and their verification.

This consistent methodology makes Sherlock Holmes a model of rational and analytical approach, allowing him to solve even the most intricate crimes by relying on logic and facts rather than intuition or guesswork.

The Analytical Method in The Practice of Hercule Poirot in Agatha Christie's Books.

Hercule Poirot, the famous Belgian detective created by Agatha Christie, also uses the analytical method in his investigations, paying exceptional attention to every detail that can lead to the solution of the crime. His methodology focuses on a thorough examination of all the circumstances and evidence, which allows him to solve even the most intricate crimes.

(a) Attention to Detail

For Hercule Poirot, every detail matters, every detail can lead to the truth. His analytical method is based on a deep conviction that no detail can be overlooked. Poirot examines everything from the words and gestures of witnesses to the smallest physical clues that may seem inconsequential to others, but to him, they are the key to solving the case.

Example. In the novel *Murder on the Orient Express*, Hercule Poirot is confronted with a crime committed on a train trapped in the snow. The murder took place in a confined space where all the passengers seemed innocent. Poirot scrutinizes the footprints in the snow outside the window - those that point to a possible fugitive, but they seem too obvious. He sees this as the first inconsistency. But his attention to detail reveals even more when he begins to interview the passengers. Small inconsistencies in their stories, and minor details in their behavior, such as awkward pauses or avoidance of direct answers, do not escape his observant eye. A seemingly insignificant discrepancy in the way the passengers describe the moment when the murder took place becomes an important thread to which Poirot clings.

Details that others might not have noticed, such as the posture of a body or an unusually placed item in a compartment, turn into crucial clues. And when Poirot finds a small clue - an object accidentally dropped at an inopportune moment - it becomes the key to unlocking the conspiracy. This methodology, in which attention to the smallest details plays a crucial role, raises Murder on the Orient Express to the level of one of the most intriguing novels in the detective genre.

(b) Psychological Analysis

Hercule Poirot pays great attention to the psychology of suspects. It is important for him to understand the inner world of each person in order to uncover the true motives and find out who is capable of committing a crime. Poirot carefully observes the behavior of suspects, their reaction to questions, their manner of communication, and how they interact with each other. Psychology is as important a clue to him as physical evidence.

Example. In the novel *Death on the Nile* Hercule Poirot is confronted with a mysterious murder committed aboard a luxury steamship crossing the waters of the Nile. The passengers are surrounded by intrigue and secret motives, everyone is hiding something important. At first glance, it seems that everyone is nice to each other, but beneath the surface lurks envy, jealousy, and a desire for revenge.

Poirot begins his psychological analysis by examining the relationships between the passengers. He notices subtle changes in their behavior when the subject of murder is raised. For example, one of the key characters, at first glance, seems indifferent to what is happening, but upon closer observation, Poirot catches the smallest nuances of her behavior - nervous gestures, and short glances to the side, which give away her true emotions. Carefully analysing how the passengers react to the death of a wealthy and powerful woman, he realizes that many of them may have had motives for the crime.

Poirot also pays attention to how suspects react to his questions. Some are immediately defensive, others try to avoid the subject, and some try too hard to look innocent. Each of these subtle psychological signs helps Poirot build a more accurate picture of what is going on. He links emotional reactions to possible motives - love, jealousy, or financial interests. And as a result of his subtle psychological analysis, the confusing situation gradually becomes clearer.

(c) Interviewing

Hercule Poirot interviews suspects and witnesses, asking seemingly simple but very precise questions. His methodology is based on identifying contradictions in testimony and looking for subtle inconsistencies that may reveal lies or ulterior motives. Poirot skillfully leads people to frank conversations, even if they are initially reluctant to share important details. He carefully observes the reactions of his interlocutors, analysing not only words but also gestures, tone of voice, and emotional expressions to better understand what lies behind the words.

Example. In the novel The Murder of Roger Ackroyd, Hercule Poirot is confronted with a mysterious murder in a small English village. The villagers, as well as the family members of the murdered man, at first glance, give quite logical and consistent testimony. However, Poirot, using his exceptional interviewing skills, quickly realizes that many of these accounts are lies and deliberate concealment of facts.

He conducts a series of interviews with various family members and villagers, asking carefully selected questions. During these conversations, Poirot uses not only direct questions but also leading questions that bring to light internal contradictions in the testimony. One family member becomes nervous when asked about his whereabouts on the night of the murder, another tries to sidestep the topic of finances, which becomes too uncomfortable. Carefully analysing each reaction, Poirot slowly but surely uncovers the web of lies being woven by those around him.

(d) Systematization of Facts

Hercule Poirot gathers information, carefully records all the details, and compares them to reveal a logical connection between individual events. This approach helps him to build a complete picture of what is happening, where every detail takes its place, and separate fragments of information gradually add up to a single solution. Poirot does not hurry to draw conclusions until he is convinced that all the facts support his theory.

Example. In the novel Cards on the Table, Hercule Poirot encounters an unusual case where card games and the behavior of the participants play a key role. During a party organized by the eccentric Mr. Shaitana, one of the guests is murdered and all the suspects are present in the room. Each of them had a chance to commit the crime, but the clue is hidden in the way they behaved at the card table.

Poirot systematizes all the facts, from the details of the murder itself to the nuances of the behavior of the participants in the game. He carefully analyses how each player made decisions, what strategies he used, and what mistakes he made - this allows him to understand the psychology of each suspect. Poirot uses his observations of how people behave in tense moments, matching this with their reactions to the murder.

The card game becomes a metaphor for crime, and Poirot skilfully links behavior at the gaming table to possible motives. Systematizing these observations, he discovers that the careless movements, hidden intentions, and emotional outbursts of the players provide important clues. The cards people hold and their actions during the game, like puzzles, add up to a complete picture of the crime.

Chapter 5. Deductive Method

"All men are mortal. Socrates is a human being. Therefore, Socrates is mortal."
Aristotle's Analytics One (one of the six treatises that make up the "Organon")

Definition:

The deductive method is a method of logical reasoning in which specific conclusions logically follow from general premises. If the premises are true and logically consistent, then the conclusions drawn from them will also be true.

Landmark figures:
Aristotle, René Descartes, Immanuel Kant.

Application:
The deductive method is widely used in philosophy, mathematics, logic, and natural sciences, being the basis for building theories and proving statements. The essence of the deductive method is that specific conclusions are deduced from general principles or axioms, which logically follow from the proposed initial data. This method allows structuring arguments so that each next step is strictly justified by the previous one.

The deductive method provides logical consistency, eliminates the possibility of contradictions, and helps to build rigorous and sound reasoning, which makes it an indispensable tool in various fields of knowledge.

The Main Components of the Deductive Method

(a) General Premises. In the deductive method, general premises are initial statements or axioms that are accepted as true without the need for proof. They are the foundation on which the entire logical chain of reasoning is built. It is their accuracy and clarity that determines the consistency and validity of the conclusion. These premises must be formulated in such a way as to exclude doubt since they serve as the starting point for all subsequent conclusions.

In mathematics, for example, axioms such as "only one line can be drawn through two points" become the basis for all geometric conclusions. In philosophy, the deductive method may be based on well-known facts or universal principles. These statements, without requiring proof, provide the basis for further deduction of logical consequences.

(b) Logical Reasoning. In the deductive method, logical reasoning is the key process by which specific conclusions are derived from general premises. This process is based on the strict application of the laws of formal logic. Logical reasoning must be absolutely consistent, avoid contradictions, and strictly follow principles such as the law of non-contradiction and the law of the excluded third.

Each step in the logical chain should be clear, justified, and derived from the previous statements. It is important that each intermediate conclusion is correctly formulated and logically related to the initial premises. Breaking the sequence or relying on questionable steps can destroy the entire logical construction and make the conclusion unreliable.

Logical reasoning is the heart of the deductive method, allowing a smooth transition from general statements to specific conclusions, and maintaining the structure of reasoning throughout the analysis.

(c) Specific Conclusions. Specific conclusions in the deductive method are conclusions that follow logically from the initial premises and intermediate steps of reasoning. These conclusions are the end result of a logical chain where each step is justified by previous statements. If the reasoning was constructed correctly and the premises were true, the conclusions will inevitably be true.

Unlike other methods, in the deductive process, conclusions do not require further verification through experience or empirical data. Their truth is guaranteed by the fact that they strictly follow general premises and logical rules. For example, if the statements "all men are mortal" and "Socrates is a man" are true, then the conclusion "Socrates is mortal" will also be true because it logically follows from these premises.

Specific conclusions in the deductive method have the character of immutable truth, provided that the initial premises were correctly chosen and the process of logical reasoning was free of errors. This makes the deductive method a strong tool for drawing accurate and reliable conclusions that do not require additional confirmation in reality.

(d) Verification. Verification in the deductive method is the process of checking the correctness of the conclusion and the logical chain by which the reasoning has been constructed. This step is to make sure that all intermediate steps and specific conclusions follow logically from the underlying premises and that all laws of logic are satisfied. Verification also involves checking the premises themselves for truth and logical consistency. If the premises are true and the logical structure of the reasoning is correct, then the conclusions are automatically considered correct. However, if at least one element of the chain is broken - either the logic is incorrect or the initial statements are incorrect - the entire conclusion may be called into question.

Verification not only guarantees the logical correctness of the process but also serves as a final check on the entire reasoning construct. It is a key step to ensure that the conclusion is not only logical but also true, based on verified and valid premises.

The Deductive Method in the Context of Philosophy

René Descartes used the deductive method, starting with the fundamental principle of his philosophy - "Cogito, ergo sum" (I think, therefore I exist). For him, this simple but fundamental statement became the undeniable truth from which he began to build his entire philosophical system. From this first, irrefutable fact, Descartes consistently developed his thoughts, applying the deductive method to deduce more complex truths. One of the key themes in his reasoning was the proof of the existence of God.

René Descartes wonders how the idea of God came into his mind. He realizes that he himself as a human being is a finite and imperfect being, while the idea of God is an image of an infinite and perfect being. Descartes concludes that such an idea could not have arisen from nothing or been generated by an imperfect mind. If a finite human being is able to think of the infinite, then the source of this idea must exist objectively and be as perfect as the idea itself. Descartes' logical chain is based on the fact that the idea of God could only have been put into his mind by a being possessing these attributes - God himself.

Aristotle is one of the founders of formal logic. In his treatise, Organon, Aristotle developed the structure of syllogisms, a form of deductive reasoning where conclusions logically follow from two or more premises. Aristotle's syllogisms are the basis for many subsequent developments in logic and the deductive method.

An example of a syllogism:
Premise 1: All humans are animals.
Premise 2: All animals are mortal.
Conclusion: All human beings are mortal.

In *The Critique of Pure Reason,* **Immanuel Kant** uses the deductive method to analyse in depth the possibilities of human cognition. In the transcendental deduction of categories, Immanuel Kant seeks to show that our minds organize and structure experience by means of a priori concepts - categories that precede any empirical knowledge. These categories, Immanuel Kant argues, are necessary for us to perceive the world sensibly.

Example.

Immanuel Kant asks a key question: how do we perceive the world around us and how are we able to organize it into structures that we can understand? In other words, what makes our meaningful perception and understanding possible? In his search for an answer, Immanuel Kant comes to the conclusion that the very process of cognition is impossible without a certain internal structure embedded in the mind before any experience.

Immanuel Kant argues that our mind possesses a priori categories, such as causality, unity, time, and space, which act as "glasses" through which we see the world. These categories are not derived from experience; they exist in the mind prior to any interaction with the external world. For example, the category of causality allows us to perceive events as related in a cause-effect way, and the categories of time and space allow us to realize that events occur in a particular sequence and within particular physical limits.

Immanuel Kant uses the deductive method to show that without these a priori categories, any experience would be chaotic and disorganized. Our perception, he argues, is structured by these concepts, which makes all knowledge and understanding possible. Immanuel Kant proves that reason is not passive in the process of cognition, but actively shapes experience by imposing its a priori structures on it.

Immanuel Kant's Analysis of the Category of Causality

1) A Priori Category

Causality, or the idea that one event causes another, is one of the a priori categories of reason that exist prior to all experience. Immanuel Kant argues that our mind originally possesses this category, and it does not arise in the process of empirical perception. This idea exists in our minds before we encounter any concrete examples of cause and effect in the world around us.

2) Experience

When we observe events such as a ball hitting a glass and the subsequent breaking of the glass, our mind automatically perceives this as a cause and effect relationship. The ball (cause) breaks the glass (effect). This connection seems obvious to us, as the mind uses the built-in category of causality to link these two events in time and space. For Kant, however, this connection is only possible because of the a priori category of causality that is already present in our minds.

3) Deduction

Immanuel Kant draws an important conclusion: causality is not just an observed relation between objects in the world, as many philosophers before him believed, but a necessary category of reason that makes possible the very perception of such relations. Without this a priori category, our minds would not be able to combine the events of hitting the ball and breaking the glass into one logically related phenomenon. We would see only two independent events incapable of explaining each other. Causality, according to Kant, is superimposed on our experience so that we can conceptualize what is happening and link it into a coherent whole.

4) Conclusion

Causality does not arise from experience; rather, it is necessary for experience to exist and for us to understand the world around us. This a priori category of the structure of the mind allows us to organize and make sense of things. Causality is one of the tools our mind uses to give events logical coherence and order.

Immanuel Kant shows that without a priori categories such as causality, our experience would be chaotic and meaningless. These categories are not derived from experience, but precede it, making our meaningful perception of the world possible. It is because of them that we are able to connect events, organize them into causal series, and understand what is going on around us.

An example of the use of the deductive method in literary works: Arthur Conan Doyle's Sherlock Holmes stories and novels.

Sherlock Holmes uses the deductive method to solve crimes. He starts with known facts and general principles, then logically deduces specific conclusions that help Sherlock Holmes solve complex cases.

An example of the use of the deductive method in the practice of Sherlock Holmes

(a) General Prerequisites

Sherlock Holmes often begins his investigations with general assumptions based on his experience and observations. For example, principles such as "All people who leave muddy footprints came from the street" or "If a person is wet, it means he was in the rain" become the starting points in his chain of logic. These premises do not require proof because they are based on common sense and easily verifiable observations.

General statements help Holmes to build further conclusions. He uses them as a foundation for analysing the specific circumstances of the case, which allows him to immediately exclude some hypotheses and focus on plausible explanations.

(b) Logical reasoning

Sherlock Holmes uses general premises for logical reasoning by applying them to specific observations. For example, if he sees wet footprints on the floor of a house, he automatically associates it with a general principle: wet footprints mean that a person has recently been outside in the rain. From this, Sherlock Holmes draws the logical conclusion that someone has recently come in from the street in the rain.

This reasoning process allows Sherlock Holmes to build logical chains where each detail takes on its own meaning in the context of the overall situation. He does not simply record observations, but instantly connects them to general principles, drawing logically sound conclusions.

(c) Specific Conclusions

Sherlock Holmes always draws his conclusions based on a careful logical analysis of the facts. For example, if Sherlock Holmes notices specific dirt on a suspect's shoes, he uses this fact to conclude that the person in question has been to a certain place where such dirt can be found. Every detail is important to Sherlock Holmes, and he has a knack for linking seemingly insignificant clues to specific locations or events.

The deductive method allows Sherlock Holmes not just to observe facts, but to build a chain of logical inferences that lead him to an accurate understanding of where a person has been, who he or she may have met, and what this means for the investigation. Each detail becomes part of the bigger picture, and Sherlock Holmes always uses specific clues to draw plausible and valid conclusions.

(d) Verification

Sherlock Holmes does not stop at the first conclusions he draws. He always verifies their truth by comparing them with other facts and observations. This verification stage allows Sherlock Holmes to make sure that his conclusions are logically consistent and justified. If at any stage the logical chain is broken or contradictions appear, Sherlock Holmes returns to the analysis to eliminate errors and confirm his conclusions. Each of his theories is tested for consistency and validity.

Chapter 6. Empirical Method

"There is nothing in the mind that was not previously in the senses."
John Locke's "Experience of Human Reasoning"

Definition:

The empirical method is a research method based on observation, experience, and experiment.
The empirical method involves collecting data through sense perception and using that data to form and test hypotheses.

Landmark figures:
Francis Bacon, John Locke, David Hume.

Application:
The empirical method is actively used in sciences and philosophy to comprehend knowledge about reality. It is based on observation and experimentation, through which the researcher comes to understand the regularities of the world. This method makes it possible not only to create theories but also to verify them on the basis of facts obtained in the course of practical experience. Empirical data become the basis for scientific conclusions, helping to substantiate ideas and hypotheses with a high degree of reliability.

The Main Components of the Empirical Method

(a) Observation is the first and key stage of the empirical method, where the researcher systematically and objectively studies natural or social phenomena. It involves the careful and purposeful study of an object without interfering with its nature. At this stage, it is important to maintain clarity and objectivity so that the data collected reflects reality without distortion.

Observation can be conducted both in a natural environment, where phenomena unfold without the researcher's participation, and in controlled experimental conditions. It is the quality of observations, their accuracy, and completeness that set the basis for the next steps of empirical research, influencing the correctness of conclusions and the construction of further hypotheses.

(b) Data Collection. The observation phase is followed by data collection, where all findings need to be carefully recorded and documented. This process includes recording the results of observations, experiments, and tests. Data collection serves as the basis for further analysis and hypothesis formation. For the successful application of the empirical method, it is important that the data are collected with maximum accuracy and completeness, taking into account all possible factors that can affect the phenomenon under study.

In various sciences, this process may involve measuring physical parameters, recording phenomena, or documenting experimental results in detail. The correct systematization of data at this stage determines the accuracy and validity of the conclusions that will be drawn later.

(c) Formulation of Hypotheses. Based on the data collected, the researcher formulates assumptions or hypotheses that explain the observed phenomena. Hypotheses are tentative explanations that need further testing. They must be specific and testable enough to be subjected to empirical testing.

This stage requires critical thinking and the ability to identify possible patterns, even if data are limited. Hypotheses become the basis for further experiments and observations, and their testability is a key criterion to move towards accurate and valid conclusions.

(d) An Experiment is a controlled method of hypothesis testing in which the researcher actively intervenes in the process and creates certain conditions in order to observe the response of an object. An experiment requires that the conditions be precisely defined and reproducible so that the results can be repeated. This stage provides an opportunity to investigate the relationships between phenomena and test the assumptions made on the basis of observations.

The empirical method is often based on experiments because they allow you to control variables and isolate the influence of individual factors. Through experiments, it is possible to obtain more accurate data, determine causes and effects, and test whether a hypothesis corresponds to reality.

(e) Data Analysis. After the experiments and observations have been completed, the data analysis stage comes where all the results obtained are processed and systematized. This process involves identifying patterns, evaluating hypotheses, and establishing cause and effect relationships. To achieve accuracy, various statistical methods and models can be used to help extract meaningful conclusions from the body of information.

Data analysis requires objectivity and rigor to exclude subjective interpretations and to be based solely on facts. Proper analysis helps not only to confirm or refute hypotheses but also to see deeper connections between phenomena, which makes it possible to draw valid scientific conclusions.

(f) Conclusions and Theories. In the last stage of the empirical method, conclusions are formed on the basis of the data analysis carried out and theories are developed to explain the phenomena under investigation. Theories are generalizations that cover a wider range of phenomena than the original hypothesis and become part of scientific knowledge. They not only explain known phenomena but also make it possible to predict future outcomes and events.

It is important that conclusions and theories are based on verified data and are sufficiently sound to withstand criticism and further testing. This makes the empirical method a reliable tool for discovering reality and expanding scientific understanding of the world.

The Empirical Method in the Context of Philosophy

John Locke, in his *Experience of Human Reasoning*, argues that all human knowledge originates in experience. He distinguishes two types of experience that shape our understanding of the world: sensation (external experience), which we receive through our senses, and reflection (internal experience), which includes our awareness of internal thought processes. According to John Locke, empirical data - whether external sensations or internal reflection - play a key role in the construction of knowledge and understanding of the world.

John Locke rejects the idea of innate knowledge, insisting that all our ideas and concepts are the result of our interaction with the surrounding reality and our own thinking. Thus, his philosophy emphasizes the central role of the empirical method in knowledge, making experience the basis for all knowledge about the world and ourselves.

David Hume developed the ideas of empiricism, arguing that our knowledge of cause and effect is born solely from experience. In his writings, he analyses human understanding in depth, showing that all our certainty that one event causes another is the product of observation, not innate knowledge. For David Hume, the world is like a river in which every current can only be predicted when you have already observed its movement. He emphasizes that empirical observation is the foundation of all our knowledge of the world, and without it, any conclusions will be rootless, like a plant that has never seen the sun.

Francis Bacon laid the foundation for the method of induction, emphasizing that scientific knowledge can grow like a tree rooted in empirical observation and experimentation. He criticizes the traditional methods of Aristotelian logic, which built knowledge like castles in the sand, detached from real experience. Instead, Bacon proposes an empirical approach where observation of nature becomes the starting point of inquiry. His work became the foundation of the scientific method, which relies on experience and experimentation rather than abstract inferences.

In *The New Organon*, Francis Bacon formulates a method in which the researcher first immerses himself in the observation of phenomena, like a scientist studying nature through a magnifying glass. Then, step by step, he moves from particular observations to the formation of general principles and theories. This was a radical step forward - Bacon suggested that scientists study the world directly, through its manifestations, rather than through the mediation of outdated logical schemes.

The Empirical Method in Literary Works: Stories and Novels of Arthur Conan Doyle's Sherlock Holmes

The main character, Sherlock Holmes, uses the empirical method to investigate crimes. Sherlock Holmes observes people's behavior, collects evidence, and conducts experiments to test his hypotheses. His conclusions are based on careful analysis of empirical data.

An example of the use of the empirical method in the practice of Sherlock Holmes:

(a) Observation

For Sherlock Holmes, what to others remains unnoticed becomes a key detail. For example, he can pay attention to the dirt on the suspect's shoes and, by its character, determine where the person has been. Or the odor of tobacco in a room, barely perceptible to the rest of us, will clue Sherlock Holmes into who has been here recently. His eyes are the instrument through which he discovers a hidden reality where every detail carries significance.

(b) Data Collection.

Sherlock Holmes is a meticulous collector of evidence. Every detail, be it a soil sample, a fingerprint, or a forgotten document, comes into his field of vision and becomes part of the big picture. He meticulously records everything that might matter - from insignificant minutiae to key evidence, analysing it with cold precision. Sherlock Holmes might take soil samples from a suspect's boots, compare them to the soil at a crime scene, or examine a letter to find hidden messages in it. His data collection process turns chaotic traces into a clear and understandable system ready for further analysis.

(c) Formulation of Hypotheses

After carefully gathering evidence, Sherlock Holmes begins to construct hypotheses as if he were arranging pieces on a chessboard. He analyses every detail and creates possible scenarios of what could have happened. For example, if Sherlock Holmes finds dirty footprints on the window sill, he hypothesizes that the criminal entered the house through the window. His hypotheses are not random - they follow logically from the facts he has already gathered. He builds versions, exploring how each element might connect to another until the most plausible explanation emerges.

(d) Experimentation

Sherlock Holmes does not limit himself to theory - he actively tests his hypotheses through experiments. In his arsenal - a set of scientific methods that allow him to confirm or deny his assumptions. For example, if an unknown substance is found at a crime scene, Sherlock Holmes conducts a chemical experiment to determine its composition. His office becomes a laboratory where he uses reagents to reveal hidden connections between evidence. The experiments provide Sherlock Holmes with accurate data to help him build a consistent picture of the events and confirm the truth of the hypotheses.

(e) Data Analysis

After conducting experiments and collecting all the evidence, Sherlock Holmes proceeds to the most important stage - analysing the data. He begins to build a chain of logically connected facts as if assembling a mosaic, where each fragment finds its place. Sherlock Holmes uses his vast experience and knowledge to interpret the collected information, revealing patterns that at first glance may have gone unnoticed. Analysing the results of experiments, witness testimony, and evidence, he gradually builds up a coherent picture of what happened, revealing the truth where others see only chaos.

(f) Conclusions and Theories

Sherlock Holmes always bases his conclusions on a careful analysis of data, making each conclusion the result of sound logic and actual observation. He does not rely on guesswork -

each of his conclusions is tested by experiments and observations, allowing him to uncover hidden details and establish connections between seemingly unrelated facts. This precise and methodical approach helps Sherlock Holmes solve the most intricate cases, finding solutions where others fail to see them. His conclusions turn into clear theories that explain events with immutable logic and leave little room for doubt.

In contrast, the Sherlock Holmes books often feature Inspector Lestrade, representing the official police. Unlike Sherlock Holmes, Lestrade rarely uses the empirical method, relying more on intuition, hunches, and superficial clues. His approach is often superficial: he does not delve into details, he does not analyse thoroughly, and therefore his investigations are often ineffective. Lestrade often jumps to conclusions that lead to mistakes - arresting the innocent and missing the real culprits.

The contrast between Sherlock Holmes' methodical approach and Lestrade's intuitive actions emphasizes the importance of the empirical method. Where Sherlock Holmes solves complex mysteries through precise observation, analysis, and experimentation, Lestrade, ignoring the scientific approach, fails to deal with confusing cases. This shows that only the scientific approach of Sherlock Holmes is able to reveal hidden truths and lead to correct conclusions, confirming the superiority of the empirical method in crime investigation.

Chapter 7. Phenomenological Method

"Perception is not only the collection of data but also the act through which we give meaning to the world."
Maurice Merleau-Ponty's "The Phenomenology of Perception"

Definition:

The phenomenological method is a research method aimed at describing and analysing subjective experience and consciousness.

The phenomenological method aims to study phenomena as they directly manifest themselves in consciousness. It involves the complete elimination of preconceived assumptions and existing theories so that the researcher can perceive phenomena in their pure, genuine form. The phenomenological approach requires one to set aside all pre-established ideas and simply observe how phenomena manifest themselves in one's experience, seeking to understand their essence through direct perception.

Landmark figures:
Edmund Husserl, Martin Heidegger, Maurice Merleau-Ponty.

Application:
The phenomenological method is widely used in philosophy, psychology, and social sciences to study the structure and content of consciousness. It helps to study such aspects as perception, thinking, emotions, and intentionalism - the orientation of consciousness towards certain objects. This method allows phenomena to be described and analysed in

such a way as to reveal their essential characteristics. By delving into subjective experience without preconceived theories, the researcher can understand how phenomena manifest themselves in their purest form and how they are perceived by consciousness.

The Main Components of the Phenomenological Method.

(a) Epoché. Epoché is the methodological suspension of judgment about the existence of the external world in order to focus on direct experience. This component of the method is to temporarily set aside any assumptions about the reality of external objects and focus on how phenomena manifest themselves in consciousness. The importance of epoché is that it allows the researcher to free himself or herself from preconceived attitudes and begin the study with a "clean slate." It is a kind of "stopping" of thinking about the external world that helps the philosopher or psychologist discover the pure structure of experience, freeing perception from the influence of external factors and theories. Epoché allows us to consider phenomena as they are given, without imposing an external interpretation on them.

(b) Intensionalism. The principle of intensionalism states that consciousness is always directed toward something, whether it be objects of the external world, ideas, or inner experiences. This means that consciousness is never passive or empty - it is always connected to some object or phenomenon. Intensionality emphasizes the deep relationship between the subject (the bearer of consciousness) and the object (what is conscious), making the analysis of consciousness inseparable from the analysis of the phenomena to which it is directed.

This component of the phenomenological method is particularly important for understanding how we perceive reality. When we look at a tree, think about the past, or feel an emotion, our consciousness is always "directed" toward these objects of experience. Intensionality helps the researcher understand how phenomena enter the field of consciousness, how they are realized, and how they structure our experiences.

(c) Eidetic Reduction. Eidetic reduction is a process aimed at isolating the essential characteristics of a phenomenon by abstracting it from incidental and individual features. This method allows us to move from concrete examples to the "eidos" - the essence of the phenomenon. The essence of eidetic reduction is to focus on those features that define the phenomenon, making it exactly what it is and distinguishing it from all other phenomena.

For example, if we analyse a chair, we abstract away from its color, shape, and material to focus on its essential function of being an object designed for sitting. This exercise allows us to see the "pure" form of the chair, and its eidos, revealing the essential purpose of the object. In this way, eidetic reduction helps the researcher to penetrate into the underlying nature of phenomena, cutting away all that is accidental and temporary in order to get to their essence.

(d) Descriptive Analysis. This stage of the phenomenological method involves a detailed description of phenomena as they appear in consciousness, avoiding interpretations and preconceived theories. The researcher seeks to reflect the phenomenon as the subject perceives it, without imposing any theoretical views or assumptions. Descriptive analysis focuses on the direct perception of phenomena in order to convey them in their purest form, without abstractions or dogmas.

This approach helps to avoid the distortions that can arise when interpreting experience through the prism of already existing concepts. The phenomenologist tries to "purify" perception from any external influence and create an objective basis for understanding subjective experience by conveying at maximum accuracy how the phenomenon is represented in consciousness.

(e) Understanding Subjectivity. This component of the phenomenological method focuses on exploring experience from the subject's perspective, taking into account the subject's unique experiences and perceptions. Phenomenology emphasizes how each person perceives and interprets the world around them, making subjectivity the central object of study. Understanding subjectivity means recognizing that every experience is unique and individual, whether it is the perception of external objects or internal experiences.

This approach allows the researcher to penetrate deeper into the personal worlds of people, considering their perception as the most important aspect of existence. Phenomenology does not seek to impose universal interpretations, but to reveal how each person conceptualizes his or her reality and how his or her consciousness forms this unique picture of the world.

Phenomenological Method in the Context of Philosophy.

Edmund Husserl is the founder of phenomenology. His work, beginning with Logical Investigations and continuing through to his later writings, was aimed at creating a new philosophical methodology that could provide a deeper understanding of the structure of human experience. Edmund Husserl believed that consciousness is an active force that is always directed toward something, whether it is an object of the external world or an inner experience. He introduced the concept of intentionality, which states that consciousness is never 'empty', it is always connected to the phenomena it perceives or is directed towards. This was one of the key aspects of his philosophy: to investigate not only consciousness itself but also how it interacts with the world through perception.

To investigate this process, Edmund Husserl proposed the method of epoché, a methodological "suspension" of judgments about the existence of the external world. He believed that in order to understand the structure of experience, one must temporarily abandon any assumptions and theories about the reality of external objects. Epoché allows a philosopher to view phenomena "as they are" by focusing on their immediate manifestation in consciousness. This method makes it possible to see phenomena as they are given to our perception, without superimposing on them previously established ideas and concepts.

In addition, Edmund Husserl introduced the concept of eidetic reduction, a process by which we can abstract from the accidental and individual characteristics of a phenomenon to get to its essence, or "eidos". Eidetic reduction helps to isolate what makes a phenomenon that particular phenomenon. For example, if we analyse a chair, we must set aside its specific physical characteristics (color, material) and focus on its essential function of being an object for sitting.

Edmund Husserl's phenomenological method is to describe in detail how phenomena manifest themselves in consciousness, what he calls descriptive analysis. It is important not to interpret these phenomena through the prism of existing theories or scientific explanations, but to try to describe them "in their pure form," as they are given in our perception. This makes phenomenology unique among other philosophical trends, as it strives for the purest possible perception of experience, free from preconceived notions.

Martin Heidegger, a disciple of Edmund Husserl, applied the phenomenological method to analyse the most fundamental philosophical theme - being. In his key work, Being and Time, Heidegger delves into the existential structures of human existence, offering a radically new understanding of being.

One of Heidegger's central questions is how man exists in the world and how he realizes his being. He introduces the concept of Dasein, a term that describes man's "existence" or "being-there". Dasein, according to Heidegger, is a mode of human existence that is characterized by an awareness of one's existence and the need to make choices in the context of the finitude of life.

Heidegger explored existential structures such as care (Sorge), which, in his view, is the basic defining moment of human existence. Care encompasses both man's relation to the world and his relation to the future, and expresses the fundamental tension between what man already is and what he can become.

Another important theme is being-to-death (Sein-zum-Tode), which Heidegger interprets as the realization of the finitude of existence. This awareness of death gives life a special meaning, forcing one to conceptualize one's actions and life choices in the context of their finitude. According to Heidegger, understanding death is the key to authentic existence - the ability to live fully, accepting one's finitude.

Another significant category in his analysis is temporality (Zeitlichkeit). Heidegger argues that human existence is inherently temporal, and we experience our existence through the lens of time. Past, present, and future are inextricably linked in consciousness, shaping our understanding of being. Temporality, according to Heidegger, is the basis through which human beings experience their lives and build relationships with the world.

Applying the phenomenological method, Heidegger explores not just abstract being, but concrete, deeply personal aspects of human existence. He describes the experience of being as a process in which man is constantly confronted with the necessity of choice, responsibility for his life, and realization of his finitude.

Maurice Merleau-Ponty further developed phenomenology by focusing his attention on perception and bodily existence. In *The Phenomenology of Perception*, he explores how the body and the immediate perception of the world shape our understanding of reality. For Merleau-Ponty, perception is not simply a passive reflection of the world in consciousness, but an active and deeply bodily process through which one interacts with the environment.

Merleau-Ponty introduces the concept of bodily intentionality, emphasizing that our body is not just a physical object, but an active subject directed at the world. Man does not perceive the world as something external and detached, but experiences it through the body, which is always included in the process of interaction with the environment. Perception for him is the primary experience on which all subsequent reflection is based. For example, when we see a tree, we perceive it not just as an image in our consciousness, but as something real that we can interact with - go up to it, touch it, feel its texture.

Merleau-Ponty argues that perception precedes any rational explanations and theories. Our bodily existence becomes the basis for perceiving the world, and perception is the way through which we immerse ourselves in reality. It is the body that is the "point of view" of the world through which one experiences one's relationship with space, time, and other people.

The phenomenological method reveals the essential characteristics of phenomena, exploring intentions and structuring experiences without preconceived assumptions. This method helps to gain a deeper understanding of a person's inner world and experience, revealing its unique and universal aspects. Examples from the works of Virginia Woolf and Edmund Husserl illustrate how the phenomenological method is applied to analyse and describe complex experiences and structures of consciousness.

An Example of the Use of the Phenomenological Method in the Novel Mrs. Dalloway

The novel *Mrs. Dalloway* (1925) by Virginia Woolf is one of the most famous works of modernist literature, in which the author uses a phenomenological approach to depict the inner world of her characters. Virginia Woolf creates a unique literary space where subjective experiences, thoughts, and perceptions become central elements of the narrative. This novel is a vivid example of using the technique of "stream of consciousness", which allows the reader to penetrate into the depths of the character's consciousness and see the world through their eyes.

(a) Focus on Subjective Experiences. Virginia Woolf emphasizes how her characters perceive and interpret the world around them, immersing the reader in their inner world. In her novel *Mrs. Dalloway*, the plot revolves around Clarissa Dalloway's ordinary day as she prepares for a party, but Woolf does not simply describe external events revealing the heroine's underlying thoughts, memories, and emotional reactions to everyday moments. Through this phenomenological approach, Woölf shows how Clarissa's inner world is saturated with thoughts about time, life, and her relationships with others.

For example, a simple act such as buying flowers becomes a trigger for Clarissa to reflect on her past and present. Through such everyday episodes, Woolf emphasizes that the significance of events is determined not so much by their objective importance as by how they are perceived by the protagonist. Clarissa's world is not just a physical reality, but a multi-layered space of her consciousness, where every moment of life has meaning and significance through the prism of her feelings and memories. Woolf thus shows that the subjective perception of events, even the simplest ones, is the key to understanding the inner reality of a person.

(b) Stream of Consciousness Technique. In the novel *Mrs. Dalloway*, Virginia Woolf uses the stream of consciousness technique to convey the continuous flow of thoughts, feelings, and experiences of the characters. This technique helps to reveal the complexity and multi-layered nature of the human mind, where memories, emotions, and current events are intertwined in a single stream of consciousness. For Woolf, stream of consciousness becomes the medium through which the reader is immersed in each character's subjective experience, observing their inner world as it unfolds.

Clarissa Dalloway and Septimus Warren Smith's stream of consciousness gives us the opportunity to see how their thoughts flow ceaselessly, jumping from one topic to another. Associations and memories surface in their minds, and emotions and reflections are unexpectedly intertwined with current events. This creates a sense of presence for the reader and allows for a deeper understanding of their inner conflicts and emotional states. With this technique, Virginia Woolf reveals not only the external actions of her characters but also those hidden psychological and emotional processes that shape their perception of the world.

(c) Perception of Time and Memory. Virginia Woolf in *Mrs. Dalloway* pays special attention to the perception of time, presenting it not as a sequential chain of events but as a subjective and personal experience dependent on the memory and perception of the characters. In her novel, time is not just the works of a clock, but the experiences of the characters that unite past and present in their minds. Memories of the past play an important role in shaping the present for Clarissa and other characters. They often return in thought to the events of their lives, comparing them to the present and reliving them in their memories.

Clarissa Dalloway, for example, often delves into memories of her youth, recalling relationships with friends, love experiences, and key moments that shaped her as a person. These memories intertwine with current events in her life, creating a complex and layered picture of time. The past and the present coexist in Clarissa's mind, forcing her to revisit her life choices again and again and find meaning in them. In this way, Woolf shows that time in human perception is not linear - time lives in our memory, influencing our perception of the present and shaping the inner world of the characters.

(d) Depicting the Inner World of Other Characters. Virginia Woolf does not limit herself to exploring the inner world of Clarissa Dalloway - she also delves deeply into the psyche of other characters such as Septimus Warren Smith, a former soldier suffering from post-traumatic stress disorder. Septimus' consciousness is presented as chaotic and fragmented, reflecting his deep mental anguish and sense of alienation from the world around him. Septimus' inner world is full of anxieties, hallucinations, and painful memories that create a tense and destructive picture of his mental state.

Virginia Woolf shows how the difference in perception of reality between the characters leads to a gulf in their communication and understanding. While Clarissa outwardly leads a quiet and measured life, her inner reflections on the meaning of existence and death echo Septimus's tragic perception of reality. Although their lives seem quite different, they are united in their philosophical reflections on the finitude of human existence. Through the contrast of these characters, Virginia Woolf emphasizes that the outside world can deceptively conceal inner conflicts, and mental anguish often remains invisible to others.

Chapter 8. Materialist Method

"Genesis determines consciousness."
Karl Marx's *"Toward a Critique of Political Economy"*

Definition:

The materialistic method is an approach to research that is based on the assumption that matter is the primary reality and that consciousness and all mental phenomena are the result of material processes.
The materialistic method emphasizes material conditions and their influence on social and natural phenomena.

Landmark figures:
Karl Marx, Friedrich Engels, Georgy Plekhanov.

Application:
The materialist method is used in philosophy, economics, sociology, and historical sciences to analyse and explain social, economic, and natural phenomena through the prism of material conditions and processes. This method is used to study the development of society, economy, science, and technology.

The Main Components of the Materialist Method

(a) Materiality. The materialist method is based on the principle of materiality, which states that all phenomena, both natural and social, have material conditions and processes as their basis. This means that all reality, including human consciousness, derives from material factors. Materialism rejects the supernatural or spiritual origin of the world and asserts that the world exists independently of our perception.

Thus, the study of reality is to analyse the physical and objective conditions that shape phenomena and processes.

(b) Dialectical materialism. This component is a methodological approach that combines dialectics and materialism to analyse change and development in nature and society. Dialectics assumes that all phenomena are in constant motion and interaction, subject to contradictions and change. In dialectical materialism, development occurs through the struggle of opposites, the resolution of conflicts, and the transition from one state to another, a higher state. This approach helps to explain the evolution of natural phenomena, social structures, and historical processes through the prism of material factors.

(c) Historical materialism. Historical materialism is the application of the materialist method to the analysis of the development of society. It is based on the assertion that human history is determined by changes in the material conditions of life, primarily production relations and economic structures. Historical materialism explains the change of formations (e.g., slave-holding, feudal, capitalist) through the development of productive forces and class struggle. This component allows us to understand how material interests and social relations influence historical events and changes in society.

(d) Critique of Idealism. The materialistic method rejects idealistic concepts that assert the primacy of consciousness or ideas in relation to material reality. Idealism views ideas, thoughts, and consciousness as fundamental to understanding the world. Materialism, on the other hand, argues that consciousness is a product of material conditions, not the other way around. All forms of idealism, whether philosophical, religious, or political, are criticized because they do not, according to materialists, adequately explain reality.

(e) Economic Determinism. An important component of the materialist method is economic determinism, which asserts that it is economic relations and productive forces that determine the development of society. Economic structures form the basis of society, and the superstructure (ideology, culture, politics) emerges as a reflection of these economic relations. The development of productive forces and the mode of production influence the class structure and political institutions of society, and changes in the economy lead to changes in all other aspects of social life.

Materialist Method in the Context of Philosophy

Karl Marx developed the theory of historical materialism, analysing the development of society through material conditions and production relations. He argued that material factors, such as the economy and productive forces, play a crucial role in shaping the social structure and history of society. According to Marx, changes in modes of production - from feudalism to capitalism and beyond - determine the course of historical development, and the class struggle between exploited and exploiters becomes the driving force behind these changes.

In *Capital*, Karl Marx analysed in detail how the relationship between capital and labor shapes social structures and class relations. He showed the nature of capitalism, how labor power is turned into a commodity, and how the surplus value created by labor is appropriated by capitalists. Karl Marx shows that the economic system not only affects production but also determines social relations, politics, and culture. The economic interests of the ruling classes determine the dominant ideas and social institutions, creating inequality and oppression. This eventually leads to class conflict.

In *Anti-Dühring*, **Friedrich Engels** develops the ideas of dialectical materialism, deepening the Marxist understanding of nature and society. Friedrich Engels analyses the material foundations of both the natural world and human society, using a dialectical approach to explain their changes and development. He argues that all phenomena of nature and social life are subject to the laws of dialectics - processes of contradiction, change, and transformation that lead to evolution and transformation.

Friedrich Engels criticizes idealist concepts that place ideas and consciousness above material reality, arguing that it is material conditions that are the basis of everything. In his criticism of idealism, he shows that consciousness and ideas are reflections of the material world, not primordial conditions. Dialectical materialism, according to Engels, explains how contradictions in material conditions lead to changes in nature, society, and history. In *Anti-Dühring*, he also criticizes mechanistic approaches, insisting that everything in nature and society moves, changes, and develops and that dialectics serves as the key to understanding these processes.

Friedrich Engels was always in the shadow of Karl Marx. At the same time, if there had been no Friedrich Engels, there would have been no Karl Marx. In modern terms, Friedrich Engels, being a very rich man, was Karl Marx's sponsor and paid his bills.

Karl Marx's style of writing was dry and, to me, boring. I found his *Capital* incredibly difficult to read, and it is definitely not the book I would want to read again. I still wonder how I got through it. I believe it was because Friedrich Engels was in the process of revising and preparing for publication the second and third volumes of *Capital*, which were published after Karl Marx's death in 1883.

Unlike his friend, Friedrich Engels wrote easily, incredibly easily! His style was beautiful and his thoughts were clear. Reading Engels' books gave me real pleasure. I remember *The Origin of the Family, Private Property, and the State in Relation to Lewis G. Morgan's 'Ancient Society'* which I devoured in just a few days.

Speaking of the materialist method, I would also like to mention **Georgy Plekhanov**, who developed the ideas of dialectical and historical materialism in Russia. In his works, he analysed historical development and the role of material conditions in the formation of social and political structures.

The materialist method is an important tool for analysing and explaining social, economic, and natural phenomena through the prism of material conditions and processes. The materialist method helps to explore the impact of material conditions on people's lives and consciousness, revealing their interrelationships and regularities. Examples from books by Karl Marx, Friedrich Engels, and Theodore Dreiser illustrate how this method is applied to analyse and critique social structures and economic relations.

An Example of the Use of the Materialist Method in Literature

An American Tragedy (1925) - one of the most famous novels by American writer **Theodore Dreiser**. In this work, Dreiser thoroughly explores the impact of material conditions on people's lives, their actions, and destinies. The novel is a vivid example of realism in literature, where the emphasis is on how economic and social factors determine the behavior and characters.

An American Tragedy tells the story of a young man named Clyde Griffiths, who was born into a poor family and witnessed from childhood the difficult life of his parents, who were busy preaching. Throughout the novel, one can see how social inequality determines the fates of the characters. Clyde is trapped between two worlds - the world of poverty from which he seeks to escape and the world of wealth to which he longs to belong.

Clyde takes a job at a hotel where he is introduced to the world of the rich and powerful. He aspires to a life of luxury, but his ambitions collide with harsh reality. When he finds himself in his uncle's factory and meets Roberta Alden, a simple working-class girl, a romance develops between them. However, Clyde soon begins dating Sondra Finchley, a girl from a wealthy family and sees this as a chance to enter high society.

Roberta discovers she is pregnant and demands that Clyde take responsibility for their future, asking him to marry her. This puts Clyde in an extremely difficult position, as he is already infatuated with Sondra Finchley. Clyde realizes that if he marries Roberta, his plans for marriage to Sondra will be ruined. Clyde makes the decision to kill Roberta in order to hide the pregnancy and remove the obstacle on the way to his dream. This decision leads to tragedy: Roberta is killed and Clyde finds himself at the center of a high-profile trial that ends with a death sentence for him.

(a) Description of social conditions.

In the novel An American Tragedy, Theodore Dreiser masterfully portrays the impact of social and material conditions on the fate of his protagonist, Clyde Griffiths.

Theodore Dreiser shows how environment, class inequality, and the desire to escape poverty shape Clyde's aspirations and actions. From an early age, he is confronted with the harsh realities of life, where success and wealth seem to be the only escape from poverty and humiliation.

Clyde's social conditions push him to desperate acts, making him dream of a better life, but also leading to tragic consequences. Through the story of Clyde, Theodore Dreiser shows how the American dream, with its cult of success and wealth, can be a destructive force, especially for those who have to fight for their place in the world.

(b) Critique of capitalist society.

Theodore Dreiser criticizes the capitalist society by portraying it as a system in which economic interests and production relations become the determining forces that shape the social structure. In An American Tragedy, Theodore Dreiser shows how the capitalist society creates underlying social inequalities where wealth and success become the measure of human worth. The writer uses Clyde's fate to expose the devastating consequences of the capitalist system in which human lives are victimized by economic ambition and class pressure.

(c) The influence of material conditions on consciousness:

Theodore Dreiser demonstrates how material conditions and economic relations shape not only people's behavior but also their consciousness. In *An American Tragedy* Theodore Dreiser shows that the desire for wealth and success, dictated by the cruel laws of capitalism forces the protagonist to make difficult decisions contrary to morality.

The characters in the novel begin to evaluate their lives and success solely through the prism of material achievements, which ultimately distorts their ideas about happiness and the rightness of actions. In the minds of the characters, the conviction is formed that the path to success and prosperity justifies any means. This choice inevitably leads to internal conflicts and tragic consequences.

I would also like to draw your attention to Theodore Dreiser's trilogy - *The Financier, The Titan, The Stoic*. In my opinion, this is the pinnacle of Dreiser's work. I am convinced that every person should read these books. This is especially true for those students who plan to go into business.

As a student, these books were some of my favorites. Theodore Dreiser's trilogy *The Financier, The Titan*, and *The Stoic* is a sweeping epic that chronicles the life and career of Frank Copperwood, a financial magnate whose fortune is based on the biography of real-life American entrepreneur Charles T. Yerkes. The three novels span several decades, showing Copperwood's rise from a simple bank clerk to a powerful financial tycoon whose life principles collide with the harsh realities of business and society.

Dreiser's trilogy is not just a story of one man's success and downfall. It is an in-depth exploration of capitalism, moral dilemmas, and the social structures that shape society. Through the life of Frank Copperwood, Dreiser shows how ambition and greed can lead to outward success, but simultaneously leave a person without true meaning and happiness.

Chapter 9. Idealistic Method

"True knowledge is knowledge of ideas, not of things."
Plato's "The Republic"

"We don't see something because it exists. It exists because we see it."
Johann Wolfgang Goethe's "Maxims and Reflections."

Definition:

The idealistic method is a philosophical approach that asserts the primacy of consciousness, ideas, and spiritual principles in explaining reality.

The idealist method is based on the assumption that the material world is derived from consciousness or spirit. Proponents of this approach argue that reality does not exist independently of our perception and that the world as we know it is shaped by our consciousness. The idealist method views reality as a reflection or manifestation of spirit, ideas, or thoughts. The material world is thus understood as secondary to consciousness, which plays a primary role in shaping all things.

Landmark figures:
Plato, Georg Wilhelm Friedrich Hegel, Immanuel Kant.

Application:
The idealist method is used in philosophy to analyse and interpret reality through the lens of ideas and consciousness. This method is used in the study of fundamental questions such as the nature of being, cognition, morality, and aesthetics. Philosophers using the idealist approach explore the world on

the premise that ideas and consciousness play a key role in shaping reality.

The idealistic method is also used to develop philosophical systems that explain the structure and functioning of the world on the basis of spiritual and intellectual principles. It allows us to view the material world as derived from higher intellectual and spiritual principles, which makes it useful for studying issues related to metaphysics, ethics, and aesthetics.

The Main Components of the Idealist Method

(a) The primacy of consciousness. The idealist method is based on the assertion that consciousness, ideas, or spirit is the primary reality on which the material world depends. According to idealism, the material world does not exist independently but is a manifestation or reflection of consciousness. This idea is directly opposed to materialism, which holds that consciousness is the result of material processes. Idealists, on the other hand, believe that reality exists only within the mind, and that understanding the world is only possible through the study of thoughts, ideas, and consciousness.

For idealists, the material world is not an autonomous, self-sufficient entity, but the result of the interaction of ideas, spirit, and consciousness. Everything that we perceive as objective reality is in reality a subjective experience or construct of the mind.

(b) Dialectics. The idealist method uses dialectics as a key tool for logical and philosophical analysis, which involves the consideration of contradictions and their resolution in order to achieve a deeper understanding of reality. Contradictions are not seen as errors or problems, but rather as the driving force of cognition and development. Idealists argue that it is through the clash and interaction of opposites that more complex and deeper aspects of reality can be revealed.

The dialectical process involves three stages: **thesis**, which presents the original idea or assertion; **antithesis**, which proposes the opposite idea or counterargument; and **synthesis**, which combines elements of both opposites, leading to a higher level of understanding. This process allows philosophers within the idealist method to analyse phenomena based on their internally contradictory nature and, through dialectical resolution, achieve a more complete view of reality.

(c) Intuitive cognition. Idealists recognize the important role of intuition and intellectual comprehension as ways of attaining true knowledge. While rational and logical thinking is important, they believe that it is not the only or highest method of understanding reality. Intuition allows one to penetrate into deeper layers of being, beyond logic and empirical research, and to grasp the truth directly, through inner awareness.

Intuitive knowledge is the direct apprehension of ideas and spiritual principles that may not be accessible through traditional methods of analysis. This knowledge does not require proof or reasoning - it is perceived as a sudden illumination or spiritual epiphany that allows one to see the world as it is, in its purest form. Thus, intuition becomes the most important tool for grasping the true nature of reality within the idealist method.

(d) Aesthetic and moral perfection. The idealistic method attaches great importance to the study of the ideals of beauty, goodness, and truth, which are regarded as the highest goals of human endeavor. Aesthetic and moral values in idealism are seen as a reflection of the highest spiritual principles that form the basis of harmonious existence.

Through the comprehension and realization of these principles, man finds inner harmony and unity with the world around him.

(e) Transcendent principles. Idealists argue that there are higher, non-material principles that guide and explain the world. Such principles as goodness, truth, beauty, and justice, exist outside time and space and are eternal. They do not depend on material conditions and determine the direction of development of both the world and man. Idealism emphasizes the importance of comprehension of these transcendent principles for understanding the essence of existence and the structure of the universe.

Idealist Method in the Context of Philosophy

Plato is one of the founders of idealism in Western philosophy. In the dialogues, Plato argues that true reality does not consist of material objects but of eternal and unchanging ideas or forms that exist independently of our sense perception. These ideas are fundamental entities that are cognized not through the senses but through intellectual contemplation, thinking, and the comprehension of reason.

One of the most famous examples of this theory is the dialogue *The Republic* where Plato describes the world of ideas in which the highest form, the idea of the good, is found. Plato views the idea of the good as the source and foundation of all other ideas, arguing that it is this idea that illuminates the mind and helps us understand the true nature of reality. The sensual world, according to Plato, is only a shadow or reflection of the world of ideas, where all physical objects are temporary and changeable copies of eternal forms. For Plato, true knowledge is not knowledge of material things, but knowledge of the world of ideas, accessible through reason and intellectual comprehension.

Immanuel Kant recognizes the importance of empirical knowledge, but in The *Critique of Pure Reason*, he argues that our experience is structured by a priori forms of sensibility (space and time) and categories of reason (such as causality, unity, and necessity). According to Immanuel Kant, the human mind does not just passively perceive the world around it, but actively shapes and organizes experience through these a priori structures.

Immanuel Kant introduces the concept of the "thing-in-itself" (or noumenon), which is a reality that exists independently of our perception and thinking. However, the "thing-in-itself" is inaccessible to our experience - we can perceive and know only phenomena, i.e. phenomena that have already passed through the filter of our sensual and rational categories. In this way, Immanuel Kant shows that although our experience is limited to phenomena, we assume the existence of a transcendent world that cannot be fully cognized. Reality, according to Immanuel Kant, is always hidden beyond the boundaries of our sense perception and rational categories, but its existence is inevitably assumed.

Georg Wilhelm Friedrich Hegel developed the idealist method by demonstrating how consciousness develops through a dialectical process of contradictions and their resolution. In his work, *The Phenomenology of Spirit,* Hegel shows that this process is the driving force behind the cognition and self-awareness of the spirit. According to Hegel, consciousness passes through a series of stages, starting from simple forms of perception to more complex levels where it encounters internal contradictions.

Hegel argues that each stage in the development of consciousness leads to new contradictions that must be overcome in order to reach a higher level of understanding. This dialectical process leads to the absolute spirit's gradual realization of its nature. Ultimately, through overcoming all contradictions, the spirit reaches absolute knowledge, which is a complete and comprehensive understanding of reality. For Hegel, this process is not just a path to knowledge, but also a means of comprehending the unity of consciousness and the world, in which the absolute spirit realizes its true nature.

The idealist method allows for a deeper understanding of the nature of being, cognition, morality, and aesthetics, emphasizing the spiritual and intellectual aspects of reality.

An Example of the Use of the Idealistic Method in Literature

The idealistic method is clearly manifested in **Johann Wolfgang Goethe's** *Faust*, in which the central character, Dr. Faust, leads an endless search for meaning and truth. He tries to comprehend the deeper aspects of human existence. Faust strives for absolute knowledge and spiritual perfection. His relationship with Mephistopheles illustrates the struggle between material and spiritual aspirations.

(a) The primacy of consciousness and spirit

Dr. Faust is the image of a scientist, a philosopher, a man who has already achieved much in the world of science and knowledge but feels emptiness and dissatisfaction. His desire for more, for what is beyond the limits of ordinary human experience, becomes the driving force of the plot.

Goethe's idealistic approach is that Faust perceives the world not as a set of physical phenomena, but as a manifestation of spiritual and intellectual forces. For him, it is not material reality that is primary, but the inner search for truth and self-knowledge. This leads him to an agreement with Mephistopheles, where he seeks not just earthly pleasures, but profound knowledge and understanding of the world. Faustus strives for spiritual development. This becomes the basis of all his subsequent actions and decisions.

(b) Dialectics and contradictions
One of the key aspects of the idealist method in Faust is the use of dialectic, a philosophical method based on the resolution of contradictions through dialogue and conflict. The relationship between Faust and Mephistopheles can be seen as a dialectical process in which opposing ideas and forces come into conflict which eventually leads to a new level of understanding.

Mephistopheles represents a material and pragmatic approach to life, offering Faust pleasure and power. Faust, on the other hand, remains essentially an idealist who seeks meaning beyond the material world. This conflict between the two forces reflects the struggle between spirit and matter, between idealism and pragmatism.

The dialectic in "Faust" manifests itself in the fact that through the resolution of these contradictions, through encountering various life situations and temptations, Faust gradually comes to a new level of understanding. He realizes that true satisfaction does not lie in the material world but in spiritual development and self-discovery.

(c) Intuitive cognition

Faustus, despite his vast knowledge and scientific achievements, seeks something that goes beyond rational and empirical thinking. He seeks an intuitive and spiritual understanding of reality that cannot be achieved through science or logic alone. This manifests an idealistic approach where intuition and spiritual insight are considered the highest forms of cognition.

In search of higher truths, Faust turns to magic, mysticism, and spiritual practices, seeking to penetrate the mysteries of the universe. He feels that true knowledge cannot be obtained only through analysis and experimentation; it requires deep intuitive perception and inner insight. His desire for intuitive cognition is manifested in his dissatisfaction with conventional scientific methods and in his desire to go beyond the limits of human capabilities.

Chapter 10. Rationalist Method

"Cogito, ergo sum" (I think, therefore I exist).
René Descartes, "Reflections on First Philosophy"

Definition:

The rationalist method is an approach to cognition and research that asserts the primacy of reason and logical thinking in the process of cognition. This method is based on the assumption that knowledge about the world can be obtained through intellectual and logical comprehension, not only through sensory experience.

Landmark figures:
René Descartes, Benedict Spinoza, Gottfried Wilhelm Leibniz.

Application:
The rationalist method is widely used in philosophy, science, and mathematics to gain knowledge and explain phenomena through logical and deductive reasoning. Based on reason, this method is used to analyse concepts, construct theories, and prove claims, allowing researchers and philosophers to reach conclusions based on the internal logic of ideas rather than empirical observations.

In philosophy, the rationalist method is used to explore issues such as the nature of being, cognition, and ethics through the logical development of arguments. In science and mathematics, it helps to formulate hypotheses, build abstract models, and prove statements ranging from mathematical theorems to philosophical concepts based on rigorous reasoning.

The Main Components of the Rationalist Method

(a) The Primacy of Reason. In the rationalist method, reason takes the central place as the key tool to cognize the world. This principle holds that the human mind has an innate capacity to grasp basic truths that cannot be deduced from experience. According to rationalism, reason alone, without reliance on sense perception, is capable of penetrating the underlying structure of reality, discovering fundamental laws and relationships.

Rationalists argue that certain knowledge - such as mathematical truths or principles of logic - exists independently of sense experience and can be apprehended through pure reflection. For example, mathematical axioms and logical laws do not require empirical verification because they are a priori and necessary to thinking itself. Reason does not merely organize experience, but is capable of formulating laws that explain the world regardless of how it is perceived.

René Descartes believed that reason provides access to "innate ideas" that are independent of experience and precede all perception. These ideas are seen as absolute and universal, capable of explaining both physical and metaphysical phenomena, including the nature of being, God, and reason itself.

(b) Intuitive and a Priori Knowledge. Rationalists recognize the existence of intuitive and a priori knowledge - knowledge that can be obtained without recourse to sense experience. A priori knowledge is characterized by the fact that it is accessible through pure thought and is independent of the perception of the external world. For example, in mathematics and logic, we can deduce certain truths based on axioms and laws of reason without resorting to experiments or observations.

A priori knowledge includes statements such as "2 + 2 = 4" or "the whole is greater than the part", which we grasp through logical reasoning, without the need for empirical verification. These truths are taken as an inherent part of the structure of thought, they are immutable and universal. An important element of a priori knowledge is its independence from changes in the surrounding world - mathematical and logical laws remain true regardless of circumstances.

Intuitive knowledge is the direct apprehension of truth without the need for detailed proof. This knowledge arises as an instant understanding or insight when the truth becomes apparent without intermediate steps of reasoning. For example, the statement "the whole is greater than its part" requires no proof because it is logically self-evident. Rationalists believe that intuition makes it possible to understand the basic principles of logic and mathematics without much thought, and serves as a basis for further conclusions.

(c) Deductive Reasoning. One of the key methods of rationalism is deductive reasoning, a process in which conclusions are logically derived from general principles or premises. In deduction, rationalists see deduction as a way of obtaining reliable knowledge that is unchanging and independent of subjective experience. This method gives confidence that if the initial premises are true, then the conclusions will be logically correct and true.

Deduction is to derive more specific conclusions from a few axioms or general truths. For example, in mathematics, this is manifested in theorem proving: starting from axioms that are considered self-evident and do not require proof, we can deductively arrive at a set of conclusions that will be strictly logically valid.

An example of deduction is proof in geometry, where, using a few basic axioms - for example, that the sum of the angles of a triangle is 180 degrees - one can derive many theorems concerning the properties of various geometric figures. Rationalists argue that this process leads to knowledge that does not change and remains true under all conditions because it is based on logic rather than observations of the changing material world.

(d) Analytical Thinking. The rationalist method involves analytical thinking, which involves breaking down complex problems into simpler components in order to analyse and solve them thoroughly. This component is based on the assumption that in order to understand any complex problem, it is necessary to break it down into parts, examine each part separately, and then, after analysing all the elements, assemble them into a coherent structure to find a holistic solution.

Analytical thinking allows rationalists to approach problems with precision and clarity. For example, in philosophy or science, a researcher may break down a broad problem into separate aspects: causes, effects, connections, and dependencies. This helps to better understand each component and reveals hidden connections between the elements of the problem, ultimately leading to more accurate conclusions.

An example of applying analytical thinking is the process of solving a complex equation in mathematics. The equation is first broken down into separate steps, each action is analysed and simplified until the final solution is found. In this way, the rationalist approach avoids confusion and error by providing a logical path to solving the problem.

This method is applicable in a wide range of fields, from logic and mathematics to philosophy and natural sciences. Decomposing the complex into the simple allows you to focus on the basic elements of the problem, which makes it more accessible to analyse and solve.

(e) Mathematical Modeling. A key component of the rationalist method is the application of mathematical principles and models to explain and predict phenomena. Mathematics, being based on strict logical rules, provides rationalists with the ability to derive precise and universal laws applicable to both physical processes and abstract philosophical problems.

Mathematical modeling allows complex phenomena of the world to be described in precise mathematical terms, which helps to understand patterns and interactions in nature. For example, disciplines such as physics or economics use mathematical models to explain the dynamics of systems, predict their behaviour, and identify cause and effect relationships. These models can range from equations describing the motion of planets to probability theories used to analyse complex events.

Rationalists value mathematics for its ability to provide irrefutable proofs and formulas that are independent of subjective observation and experience. For example, Newton's laws in physics or theorems in geometry are the result of mathematical models and proofs that can be applied regardless of specific conditions and time.

In addition, mathematical modeling helps not only to explain current phenomena but also to predict the future behavior of systems with a high degree of certainty. This makes it a powerful tool for those who seek to comprehend the universal laws that underlie both material and abstract reality.

The Rationalist Method in the Context of Philosophy

In Reflections on First Philosophy, **René Descartes** applies the rationalist method, beginning with radical doubt and reaching the undeniable statement "Cogito, ergo sum" (I think, therefore I exist). Using deductive reasoning, René Descartes builds his philosophical system by asserting the primacy of reason in knowledge.

Descartes begins with radical doubt, discarding everything that can be questioned. However, he discovers that doubt itself presupposes thinking and thinking presupposes existence. Hence, the fact of its existence as a thinking being is indubitable. Descartes concludes that if he exists as a thinking being, he can trust his rational faculties. Since reason allows him to realize his existence, reason can also be used to comprehend other truths. Descartes concludes that reason is the primary instrument of cognition and is capable of grasping fundamental truths.

An example of **Benedict Spinoza**'s use of the rational method can be found in his treatise Ethics. Spinoza's rational method is based on the use of reason and logic to deduce truths from general principles.

One key example is his proof of the existence of God. Spinoza begins by defining God as "a substance composed of infinite attributes, each of which expresses an eternal and infinite essence." He also introduces the axiom that "substance exists by itself and is independent of anything else." From these definitions and axioms, Spinoza concludes that God must necessarily exist. His reasoning is as follows: if substance exists by itself and is independent of anything else (axiom), and if God is a substance with infinite attributes (definition), then God must exist since substance by nature necessarily exists.

Spinoza further writes that since everything that exists must derive from this substance (God), all nature and all phenomena in it are expressions of the divine essence. Spinoza uses the rational method to show that the entire world is subject to logical laws derived from the nature of God. Everything that exists by necessity, and reason is the instrument for apprehending this necessity.

In *The Monadology*, **Gottfried Wilhelm Leibniz** developed the ideas of rationalism, describing the world as consisting of monads - simple, indivisible, structureless substances that are the basic units of reality. Leibniz explains the nature of monads and their interrelationships on the basis of rational principles.

Leibniz begins by saying that monads are "the true atoms of nature" and "the elements of things." Monads have no extension, form, or division; they are the simple substances that make up all of reality. Leibniz uses deduction to explain that each monad is unique and completely closed to outside influence. Since monads do not interact with each other directly, they act according to an internal principle, "preestablished harmony." This means that all monads act as if they are harmonized with each other in advance, and this harmony is established by God.

Leibniz reasoned that if monads have no physical interaction with each other, then their coordinated behavior must be the result of divine pre-establishment. He concludes that God, as the supreme monad, created the world in such a way that all monads develop in harmony with each other despite their independence.

In this example, Leibniz uses the rational method to explain the nature of monads and their interaction within a pre-established harmony. He begins with basic rational principles and through a series of logical deductions explains the complex structure of reality.

An Example of the Use of the Rational Method in a Literary Works

The novel *Invisible Man* by Herbert Wells is a story in which the rational method becomes not just a means to an end, but the main engine of the plot, which leads the hero to tragedy. The protagonist, Griffin, a scientist obsessed with the idea of invisibility, follows the path of logic and scientific inquiry, stopping at nothing. His research is precise and meticulous. He sees them as a way to transcend the boundaries of the possible and achieve the unimaginable - to become invisible. Griffin uses his intellect as a tool in pursuit of a discovery that could turn the world upside down.

The scientist's every move is dictated by cold calculation. Rational reflection leads him through complex scientific hypotheses to the ultimate goal of invisibility. This process is described in detail in the novel: Wells immerses the reader in the world of physics and chemistry, explaining how Griffin arrives at his discoveries. Everything Griffin does has a solid scientific basis. He reasons logically, avoids emotion, and focuses solely on results. Therein lies his strength and his tragedy.

The pursuit of scientific triumph overshadows reality, pushing such concepts as morality and humanity out of his consciousness. For Griffin, people are merely objects for experimentation or obstacles in his path. The rational method that led the scientist to his great discovery becomes the cause of his inner decay.

Wells shows how a mind deprived of its emotional and ethical components can lead to self-destruction. The invisibility to which Griffin had longed turns into a symbol of his total isolation from the world, from people, and ultimately from himself. His scientific achievement, which seemed the pinnacle of reason, becomes his curse. Griffin loses touch with humanity, and his logical reasoning can no longer help him find his way back.

Invisible Man is not just science fiction. It is a warning and a profound exploration of what can happen to human beings when the mind is deprived of moral control. Immorality leads to tragedy, and even the most outstanding scientific discoveries cannot justify actions that lack human feelings and morality.

Chapter 11. Critical Method

"A scientific theory can never be proved, but it can be disproved."
Karl Popper, "The Logic of Scientific Inquiry."

Definition:

The critical method is an approach to research and analysis that is based on systematically questioning, analysing, and evaluating all aspects of the subject under study.

The critical method involves the systematic use of logic, rational thought, and empirical evidence to scrutinize claims and theories. The purpose of this method is to identify weaknesses in arguments, find contradictions or errors, and strive to find true and valid conclusions. The critical method requires a rigorous analysis of each element of a theory in order to evaluate its validity and logical validity. It involves fact-checking, using evidence and empirical data, and applying logical laws to identify errors or flaws in reasoning.

Landmark figures:
Immanuel Kant, Karl Popper, Jürgen Habermas.

Application:
The critical method is used in various fields - philosophy, science, sociology, and literature - to analyse and evaluate theories, claims, and cultural phenomena in depth. In philosophy, it serves as a tool for identifying weaknesses in arguments, testing the validity of ideas, and searching for more accurate and convincing conclusions. In science, the critical

method is used to evaluate hypotheses, experiments, and conclusions based on empirical data, to identify logical fallacies, and to improve scientific knowledge.

In sociology and literature, this method helps to analyse social and cultural phenomena, to critique existing ideas and structures, and to parse texts to identify biases, contradictions, or hidden meanings. Critical examination and discussion allow not only to verify the validity of information but also to develop new approaches, improving understanding of the issues under investigation.

The Main Components of the Critical Method are:

(a) Systematic doubt. A key element of the critical method is systematic doubt - the principle that every assertion is questioned until its truth is verified and proven. This approach seeks to avoid the errors and biases that can arise when information is hastily taken on faith. Doubt is applied to all statements, including those that seem obvious or generally accepted.

The purpose of systematic doubt is to identify possible weaknesses in an argument and to test whether claims are based on reliable facts, rationale, or solid evidence. This component of the critical method was inspired by the work of René Descartes, who in his famous principle "cogito, ergo sum" ("I think, therefore I exist") called for questioning everything except the act of thinking itself. Systematic questioning helps to avoid illusions, errors, and prejudices, opening the way to more accurate and verified knowledge.

(b) Analysis and Evaluation. The critical method involves in-depth analysis and evaluation of all aspects of the subject under study, including context, arguments, and evidence. This component requires a logical and rational approach to scrutinize all sides of an issue. The aim is to assess the plausibility of arguments, their logical consistency, and their consistency with the evidence.

Critical analysis involves deconstructing arguments - breaking them down into their constituent parts to identify possible errors, inconsistencies, or contradictions. This allows us to identify weaknesses in the logic and to offer a more reasonable understanding of the subject. Arguments are evaluated on the basis of their logical consistency, adequacy of evidence, and connection to real facts, which makes the critical method an important tool for sound research and testing of theories.

(c) Empirical Verification. An integral part of the critical method is empirical testing, which involves the use of observations and experimental data to confirm or refute theories and claims. The critical approach assumes that any theory or hypothesis must be supported by facts, and if this support is lacking, the assertion requires revision or even refutation.

This component closely links the critical method to the scientific approach, where the testing of hypotheses through experience and observation is central. Theories that cannot be empirically tested are questioned and cannot be considered reliable.

(d) Dialogue and Discussion. Open and honest discussion plays an important role in the critical method because it creates a space for the exchange of views, arguments, and counterarguments. This process allows participants to identify errors, biases, and false conclusions that may not be obvious when analysed alone. Dialogue that includes different perspectives helps to deepen understanding of the problem and reach a more objective and proven conclusion.

The debate also serves as a way to test personal beliefs for validity. When a person is confronted with opposing arguments, this situation encourages them to reconsider their positions by identifying weaknesses and strengthening stronger arguments. The critical method through dialogue avoids narrow interpretations.

(e) Reflexivity is an important part of the critical method, involving self-reflection and critical examination of one's own assumptions, methods, and conclusions. It allows the researcher to be conscious of his or her approach, to revise and improve the process of learning as new evidence or arguments emerge. Reflexivity requires the ability to be self-critical, to admit mistakes, and to be willing to change one's beliefs if they are no longer consistent with new evidence.

This component of the critical method promotes continuous improvement in thinking. The researcher should analyse not only other people's arguments but also his or her own, asking: "What are my premises based on?" or "Do my conclusions correspond to new information? Reflection helps to avoid dogmatism and bias, promoting flexibility of thought and openness to new ideas.

The Critical Method in the Context of Philosophy

Immanuel Kant developed the critical method as a way of investigating the possibilities and limits of human reason. In *The Critique of Pure Reason*, he explores the structure of reason, analysing what we can know a priori and what requires empirical confirmation, determining the possibilities and limits of what can be known, and how the structures of reason shape our perception of the world.

Karl Popper is known for his writings on the philosophy of science, where he developed the concept of falsifiability as a critical method of testing scientific theories. He argued that scientific hypotheses should be testable and refutable, not just confirmable.

Popper wrote that in any science one can find many cases where hypotheses are supported but not true. The problem is that you can find many examples that agree with a hypothesis, but that does not mean that the hypothesis is true in the general case. For example, the statement "all swans are white" can be supported by many observations of white swans, but just one observation of a black swan disproves the statement.

Popper insisted that true scientific theories must be fundamentally falsifiable, i.e., it must be possible to present such observations or experiments that could disprove the theory. This is the only way to test the strength and reliability of a scientific hypothesis. If a theory cannot be disproved under any circumstances, then it is not scientific but rather belongs to the sphere of metaphysics or ideology.

According to Popper, falsifiability leads to the fact that scientific knowledge becomes more reliable and stable because a theory that has undergone many tests and has not been refuted has a better chance of being close to the truth. This does not guarantee its absolute truth, but it increases its scientific value.

Popper believed that the introduction of the thesis of the necessity of refutability leads to scientific progress. When a hypothesis is criticized and tested for refutation, it is either confirmed as having stood up to scrutiny or replaced by a new, more accurate hypothesis. Thus, science is constantly moving forward, purging its theories of errors and moving closer to the truth through the process of eliminating misconceptions.

It should be emphasized that Popper did not claim that any theory will necessarily be disproved. On the contrary, theories that undergo numerous attempts at refutation become more reliable. Truth, according to Popper, is a process, not an end state. Scientific truth is something that withstands criticism and scrutiny, remaining in line until a theory emerges that better explains phenomena and is also tested.

Jürgen Habermas has utilized the critical method in his studies of communication and social structures. In works such as *A Theory of Communicative Action*, Jürgen Habermas analyses how dialogue and discussion can be used to identify and address systematic distortions in social and political systems.

The critical method is an important tool for analysing and evaluating theories, claims, and cultural phenomena through systematic doubt, logical reasoning, and empirical verification. Examples from the works of Immanuel Kant, Karl Popper, Franz Kafka, and George Orwell illustrate how this method is applied to analyse and interpret various aspects of reality and human experience.

An Example of the Use of the Critical Method in Literary Works

In the novel ***The Trial*, Franz Kafka** creates a dark and disturbing picture by exploring important themes such as bureaucracy, absurdity, and injustice. The story centers on the life of Josef K., an ordinary bank clerk who suddenly finds himself embroiled in a ridiculous and impersonal court system. Although Josef K. does not know what he is accused of and is never given a clear explanation of his guilt, his life is gradually thrown into chaos by the relentless harassment by the state authorities.

The judicial system that Josef K. encounters is full of ridiculous rules, meaningless procedures, and soulless executors. This system seems to the hero something hostile and incomprehensible, something he cannot control or even understand. In this world, laws become an instrument of suppression rather than an instrument of justice. Joseph K. gradually realizes that he will not be able to find a logical explanation for what is happening or to achieve justice. Each attempt to understand the situation only deepens his confusion and despair. Through this story, Kafka reveals the absurdity of existence in a world where laws and rules have no meaning and where a person can be destroyed for no reason.

An example of the use of the critical method in *The Trial*:

(a) Systematic Doubt

Throughout the novel, Josef K. questions the validity and logic of the judicial system in which he finds himself. His quest to understand what he is being tried for and the nature of his alleged crime is met with a complete lack of reasonable answers. The court hearings and interrogations he faces seem ridiculous and devoid of meaning, leading him to question the very nature of justice.

Kafka uses systematic doubt as a tool to reveal the absurdity and irrationality of the judicial system. Josef K. does not simply accept his fate, he actively tries to figure out what is going on, and in this process of doubt, he is confronted with the fact that he is surrounded by an impenetrable wall of bureaucracy that defies any rational explanation.

(b) Analysis and Evaluation

Kafka, through his hero, deeply analyses the bureaucratic system, showing its irrationality and cruelty. Josef K. finds himself in a world where rules and laws exist for their own sake, not for the sake of justice or order. He sees how officials and judges, who are supposed to uphold the law, do not themselves realize what they are doing and perform their duties mechanically, without regard for human lives.

Kafka shows how bureaucracy becomes a self-perpetuating force, subjugating everything and everyone. The system that is supposed to protect people becomes a source of fear and suppression, and even those who work in it cannot escape its cruel clutches. This analysis brings to the surface the problem of alienation and dehumanization that arises under conditions of total bureaucracy.

(c) Empirical Validation.

Although the novel is allegorical in nature, Kafka uses realistic details and situations to critically analyse social and legal institutions. The descriptions of courts, interrogations, and interactions with officials are reminiscent of scenes in real life, which heightens the sense of horror when dealing with the bureaucratic system. Kafka shows that even in the real world people can face similar situations where laws and justice become abstract concepts that have no relation to real life.

The empirical test in this context is that Kafka creates a world where absurdity becomes the norm, and where reality is so absurd and inexorable that it cannot be logically explained. This reinforces the critical charge of the novel by showing that even in everyday life such situations can arise, leaving the individual helpless in the face of incomprehensible and impersonal forces.

George Orwell's *1984*.

George Orwell's novel *1984* (published in 1949) is one of the most famous and significant literary works of the 20th century, in which the author critically examines the nature of totalitarian regimes and mechanisms of social control. Orwell describes a dystopian world where political structures completely subjugate people's consciousness and freedom, destroying any manifestations of individuality and resistance. This novel is a warning of what can happen if democracy and human rights are lost.

In the novel *1984*, Orwell showed a dystopian future in which the state, represented by the Party, controls every aspect of the lives of its citizens. Totalitarianism reaches its peak in a time where technology allows for the surveillance of every move and thought of an individual. Technological surveillance and manipulation of information become the primary tools of power through which the Party suppresses freedom. Orwell wrote "1984" at a time when there was still no internet, no cell phones, and no electronic money. Yet somehow, in some unfathomable way, Orwell was able to see today and was horrified by what he saw. In the novel, Orwell showed with stunning accuracy the Party's total control over the population - what is happening today.

The central character of the novel, Winston Smith, lives in London, which has become part of the state of Oceania. This society is controlled by a Party led by Big Brother, a symbol of absolute power and omniscience. The Party rewrites history, manipulates facts, and uses propaganda to create the illusion of the only true reality. Any deviation from the official party line is punished with brutal repression. Winston, working in the Ministry of Truth, is responsible for falsifying historical records, but gradually begins to doubt the truth of the world around him.

An Example of the Use of the Critical Method in *1984*:

(a) Systematic Doubt

The main character, Winston Smith, represents a man who does not take for granted what the Party tells him. He constantly questions the veracity of the information given to him by official sources. Winston realizes that what is broadcast on television and printed in newspapers is only a version of reality that the Party has created to control society. These doubts lead him to search for the truth and try to understand what is really going on.

Winston seeks to realize that there is an alternative reality hidden from the eyes of the majority and that there is something more behind the facade of totalitarian ideology. His doubts push him to look critically at the world around him and find ways to resist.

(b) Analysis and Evaluation

George Orwell in the novel analyses and criticizes the totalitarian system, showing how it uses manipulation and control of consciousness to suppress freedom. The Party controls not only people's actions but also their thoughts, through the so-called "doublethink" - the ability to believe two contradictory statements at the same time. This allows the Party to control the mass consciousness, shape a false reality, and destroy any attempts of dissent.

Winston Smith, reflecting on the nature of the Party's power, sees how the system uses propaganda, violence, and fear to maintain its power. His analysis leads him to realize that the purpose of the Party is not to serve the people but to have absolute control over all aspects of life. Through this analysis, Orwell shows how totalitarianism destroys freedom, suppresses the individual, and turns people into wordless instruments of power.

(c) Empirical Validation

Orwell emphasizes that Winston tries to find evidence and facts that contradict the official version of events. This eagerness to check reality becomes an important element of his internal struggle. Winston realizes that without realizing the truth it is impossible to resist lies, and so he searches for facts that could confirm his doubts.

In his attempts, he encounters the lies and distortions that permeate every aspect of life in Oceania. These empirical tests, although leading to frustration and realization of hopelessness, become important to understand the depth and totality of the Party's control.

(d) Dialogue and Discussion

Winston's inner monologues and his conversations with other characters, such as Julia and O'Brien, reveal his critical views of society. Julia, Winston's mistress, represents the opposite approach to resistance - she focuses on enjoying the present moment and openly violating the prohibitions of the Party. In contrast to her, Winston seeks to understand and destroy the system itself from within.

The dialogues with O'Brien, an influential member of the Party who at first appears to be Winston's ally and then turns out to be his main enemy, play a key role in revealing the ideological depth of the novel. O'Brien, while maintaining the appearance of dialogue, actually demonstrates the full power and brutality of totalitarian control, convincing Winston that resistance is futile and the search for truth is only an illusion.

(e) Reflection

Reflection is an important aspect of the critical method used in the novel. Winston Smith is constantly reflecting on his situation, how he got into this world, and his role in it. His reflections lead to deep introspection and critical thinking about the world around him. He realizes that he lives in a society where personal freedom is destroyed and every person is under constant supervision and control. These thoughts lead him to seek a way out of this system, although he realizes the danger and complexity of this path.

Winston analyses not only the external world but also his inner experiences, trying to find a connection between his desire for freedom and the reality in which he exists. Reflection becomes an important tool in his inner struggle to maintain his humanity in the face of total repression.

I have often mentally returned to this book and to the personality of George Orwell. On the one hand, the writer was against tyranny and total control. On the other hand... In the 1990s, the documents of the IRD ("Information Research Department" (IRD) - a department of the British Foreign Office, created in 1948 to counteract communist propaganda, and at the same time collecting information about all those whom the government considered unreliable - were declassified. George Orwell voluntarily, and secretly from everyone, cooperated with this department. Among the declassified documents they found a list of 38 names compiled by Orwell, in fact - a banal denunciation of famous people who for some reason did not like Orwell. Among the people on Orwell's list were writers George Bernard Shaw and John Ernst Steinbeck, actors Charlie Chaplin, winner of several Oscars Katharine Hepburn, directors, poets, playwrights ... Each of the names, like a bright star in the sky, idols of millions. And they are all in George Orwell's denunciation. Did Orwell realize that by doing so he could destroy the careers and lives of all these people? Surely, he did, he couldn't have been unaware. From a human point of view, it was a mean stab in the back from the dark. In real life, George Orwell did what those he condemned in his books did.

Chapter 12. Existential Method

"Man is condemned to be free."
Jean-Paul Sartre's "Existentialism is Humanism."

Definition:

The existential method is an approach to research and analysis that focuses on the study of human existence, freedom, individuality, and the meaning of life. The existential method emphasizes the subjective experience, emotional experience, and personal responsibility of the individual.

Landmark figures:
Søren Kierkegaard, Jean-Paul Sartre, Martin Heidegger, Albert Camus.

Application:
The existential method is used in philosophy, psychology, and literature to analyse and understand human existence and to explore concepts such as freedom, anxiety, alienation, and the meaning of life and death. This method is used to explore a person's personal choices and actions in the context of their existence and responsibility.

The Main components of the Existential Method

(a) Subjective Experience. The existential method puts the subjective experience of a person in the center of attention, considering it as a fundamental element in the cognition of oneself and the surrounding world. In existential philosophy, individual perception and personal experiences play a key role, as through them a person learns his or her identity and builds relationships with the world. In contrast to more objective philosophical approaches, existentialism emphasizes the uniqueness of human existence, emphasizing that each person goes his or her own unique way, filled with personal meanings and values.

This component of the method explores essential human experiences - such as love, fear, loneliness, despair, and freedom of choice - as central to the formation of individual meanings. The human being in existentialism is not seen simply as part of the objective world, but as a being who gives the world personal meaning through the prism of his or her experiences and emotional experiences. The subjective experience becomes the basis for philosophical reflection, where the search for meaning and the realization of one's existence are connected with personal inner experiences.

(b) Freedom and Responsibility. Existentialism sees freedom of choice as one of the fundamental elements of human existence, like an open door before everyone, leading to an infinity of options. But along with this freedom comes the burden of responsibility for every decision made and its consequences. A person cannot shirk this burden - even if the choice is made under conditions of uncertainty, fear, or external constraints. Freedom is not just the right to go one's own way, but also the obligation to take responsibility for every move one makes.

This component of the existential method emphasizes that freedom is like the light that illuminates the path, but the shadows of decisions follow us, reminding us of the consequences. Every step, every thought becomes a choice, and no matter how limited the external circumstances, the freedom of choice always remains with the individual.

Existentialists argue that even in the most brutal and overwhelming conditions, freedom remains, if only in how one chooses to respond to what happens. Responsibility for these decisions is the price each person pays for his or her freedom, and it leaves no room for self-deception or attempts to run from the consequences.

(c) Authenticity. Existentialism raises the idea of authenticity as one of the central goals of human existence. To live authentically means to live in harmony with oneself, with one's own beliefs and values, without allowing oneself to be a prisoner of conformity or imposed norms. The existential method calls upon the individual to refuse to become a mere shadow of others' expectations and to strive for his or her own true life, built out of his or her deepest desires and aspirations.

Authenticity is an act of courage because it requires one to look inside oneself and recognize one's own principles, even if they contradict conventional standards. In a world where many voices call for following a common path, being authentic is like walking against the wind, forging your own path into the unknown.

Existentialists urge man not to succumb to the temptation of imitation and not to become a mechanical participant in society. Authentic existence requires a conscious choice in which every thought and action is based on a sincere inner striving, not on following standards. A life lived without authenticity becomes a theater in which one plays roles not written by oneself and loses oneself.

(d) Anxiety and alienation. The existential method delves into the study of anxiety and alienation, those states that arise when man realizes his absolute freedom, the finitude of existence and loneliness in the face of the world. Anxiety, in existential philosophy, is not just a negative feeling, it can be compared to the deep abyss into which a person looks when he realizes that all responsibility for his life and choices lies solely with him. This fear of the infinity of possibilities and the uncertainty of the future does not paralyze, but, on the contrary, opens the way to true existence.

Anxiety, as a state, is a sign that one is awakening to the realization of one's freedom, realizing that there are no predetermined paths and that every decision has weight and consequences. It makes one think about the finitude of life, about the fact that time is limited, and it is this anxiety about existence that can become a driving force in the search for true meaning.

Alienation in existential philosophy is a feeling of loss of connection with oneself, with others, and even with the world, as if one has become a stranger on this planet, finding no place for oneself among the usual schemes and standards. Alienation can be the result of following imposed paths, losing oneself in the hustle and bustle of life, and forgetting one's true desires and goals. This disconnection between the self and the world, between the individual and the environment, makes life feel like a meaningless existence, where connections are broken and meanings are lost.

Existentialists see these feelings not as a dead end but as an opportunity for awakening: anxiety and alienation become the key to looking at one's life from a new, deeper perspective and finding one's own path.

(e) Meaning of Life and Death. Existentialism pays particular attention to thinking about the meaning of life and death, seeing them as inextricably linked issues at the center of human existence. Human beings live in uncertainty, and one of the few absolute facts is the finitude of life. Existential philosophy does not seek to avoid this reality but rather views death as an important aspect that gives life poignancy and depth.

Existentialists do not see death as an end, but as an ever-present reminder that time is limited, and it is this realization that drives one to search for true meaning. Death is a horizon beyond which everything disappears, but its inevitability makes every moment of life meaningful. In the conditions of finitude of existence, man faces the question: how to give meaning to his life, knowing that it will end sooner or later? This question makes people search for values and goals that can justify their choices and actions.

Death, like a mirror, reflects the meaning of life: it is the realization of its inevitability that makes us think about what is important and teaches us to live not according to other people's rules, but in harmony with our own values. In this component of the existential method, philosophers urge people to be active creators of meaning, not to rely on external sources, but to determine for themselves what makes their lives meaningful and valuable.

The Existential Method in the Context of Philosophy

Søren Kierkegaard is considered one of the founders of existentialism and one of the first to explore in depth the themes of faith, freedom of choice, and personal responsibility through the lens of subjective experience. In ***Fear and Trepidation***, he examines the inner contradictions that arise in a person facing a choice that requires absolute trust and faith despite the absence of rational guarantees.

Kierkegaard, exploring the biblical story of Abraham, who was willing to sacrifice his son at God's command, emphasizes the inner struggle of man when his freedom of choice is confronted with higher, incomprehensible demands. This choice is always filled with fear and trepidation, for it requires total responsibility and a refusal to rely on external authority or universal truths.

For Kierkegaard, subjective experience plays a key role: he emphasizes that each person must decide for himself how to act in the face of uncertainty, finding meaning and guidance within himself. This choice is a personal faith that requires the greatest freedom and carries with it the greatest responsibility.

In ***Being and Time*, Martin Heidegger** deeply analyses human existence through existential categories such as care, fear, being-to-death, and authenticity. Heidegger views man not as an abstract being, but as a Dasein - a "being-there" whose existence is inseparable from time, finitude, and his engagement with the world.

One of Heidegger's key ideas is that understanding of being is possible only through the prism of personal experience and existence, through everyday interaction with the world. Heidegger emphasizes that a person constantly lives in a state of care—the realization that existence is limited, and that one must choose and take responsibility for one's actions.

Fear and being-to-death are also central to his thinking. Fear, according to Heidegger, arises when man realizes his vulnerability in the face of the finitude of existence. This leads to the thought of death, which is always present as a backdrop to human existence, causing one to reflect on one's authenticity - a life lived in accordance with oneself and not under the influence of societal norms and expectations.

As with Søren Kierkegaard, Heidegger's authenticity refers to man's ability to be true to his authentic existence, embracing freedom and finitude rather than following prescribed standards. It is only through the realization of these existential categories, Heidegger argues, that one can gain a deeper understanding of the meaning of being and one's place in the world.

In *Being and Nothingness*, **Jean-Paul Sartre** applies the existential method to deeply analyse human existence, freedom, and responsibility, offering a radical view of how man creates meaning in his life in an environment where the world itself provides no ready-made answers. Sartre argues that man does not find meaning, but creates it through his actions and choices, taking full responsibility for each action.

According to Sartre, man is immersed in an absurd and indeterminate world where there are no predetermined goals or purposes. However, it is this realization of absurdity that liberates man, for without a predetermined framework, he is condemned to freedom. This freedom gives an opportunity to create one's life like an artist creating a picture on a blank canvas, but with it comes responsibility for everything that has been created. A person chooses who to be and bears full responsibility for the results of his decisions, without the possibility of blaming external circumstances or fate.

Sartre argues that freedom is not a privilege, but a heavy burden that leads to constant anxiety and the realization that each choice shapes not only individual aspects of life but also its overall meaning. Despite the seeming absurdity of the world, human beings are capable of endowing their lives with meaning through their actions, defining their being in every choice they make.

Application of Existential Method in Literary Works

Fyodor Dostoevsky's novel *Crime and Punishment* is a profound philosophical exploration of existential themes. At the center of the narrative is Rodion Raskolnikov, a student who, driven by a complex interweaving of ideas and feelings, commits the murder of an old woman-usurer. However, behind this act lies much more than just a crime - it is an attempt to grapple with fundamental questions of freedom, responsibility, moral choice, and the search for the meaning of life.

(a) Subjective Experience

One of the key features of existential literature is the emphasis on the subjective experience of the characters. In Crime and Punishment, Dostoevsky uses this method particularly skilfully. The entire novel is imbued with Raskolnikov's inner monologues, his reflections, doubts, and anguish. From the first pages, the reader is immersed in the world of thoughts and experiences of the protagonist, who tries to justify his decision to kill the old woman. However, his reflections do not lead to calm, on the contrary, they only deepen the internal conflict. Raskolnikov hopes that the murder will free him from moral doubts and confirm his idea that he is able to transcend conventional norms for the sake of a great goal. But as the plot develops, it becomes apparent that this act does not bring him the desired liberation, but only plunges him into an abyss of suffering and alienation.

Raskolnikov's subjective experience is particularly vivid in his dreams and visions. One of the most iconic episodes is the dream of the tortured horse, which becomes a harbinger and symbol of his inner collapse. This dream, filled with cruelty and senseless pain, reflects the hero's deepest fears and doubts, raising questions about how justified his path is and where it will lead. Raskolnikov's subjective experience becomes a mirror of his soul, reflecting all the contradictions and tragedy of his situation.

(b) Freedom and Responsibility

The question of freedom and responsibility is central to Crime and Punishment. Raskolnikov, convinced of his exceptionalism and his right to transcend moral norms, decides to kill the old woman, hoping that this act will prove his freedom and willpower. He believes that the "powerful of this world" can afford such acts for the sake of higher goals and that he himself is among those chosen. This idea of the "right to crime" becomes the basis of his philosophy, but, as Dostoevsky shows, the reality turns out to be much more complicated.

After committing the murder, Raskolnikov faces unforeseen consequences. His feelings of guilt and moral responsibility begin to weigh on him more and more, shattering his original beliefs. Despite his attempts to justify his actions, the hero gradually realizes that his freedom was an illusion and that he cannot escape responsibility for what he has done. This internal conflict becomes the driving force of the plot and leads Raskolnikov to confess his guilt.

Freedom, as Raskolnikov understood it, turns out to be not a gift but a curse. He realizes that true freedom cannot be achieved through violence and violation of moral norms, and that true strength lies not in the ability to step over people, but in the ability to take responsibility for one's actions. Dostoevsky shows that the attempt to free oneself from moral obligations leads to the destruction of personality and loss of humanity.

(c) Authenticity

Authenticity is the desire to be true to oneself and to live in accordance with one's beliefs. For Raskolnikov, this question becomes particularly acute as he becomes more and more immersed in the chaos of his inner world. On the one hand, he tries to follow his ideas about freedom and the right of the strong, but on the other hand, his mental anguish and remorse show that these ideas do not correspond to his true nature.

Gradually Raskolnikov begins to realize that his attempt to live according to abstract ideas has led him to a break with himself and others. He loses touch with people and feels isolated and alien to the world. The way to authenticity for him is through recognizing his mistake and accepting the punishment. It is in this that Dostoevsky sees the possibility for the hero to find his true self - not in rejecting moral norms, but in accepting them and realizing his own weakness.

Raskolnikov's authenticity is manifested in his decision to confess and accept punishment. This act becomes a way for him to restore his lost connection to the world and to himself, to find his place in society, and to find inner peace. Dostoevsky shows that true authenticity cannot be achieved through violence and lies; it requires humility and sincerity to oneself.

(d) Anxiety and Alienation

Anxiety and alienation are integral elements of existential experience, and in Crime and Punishment, they play a key role. After committing the murder, Raskolnikov begins to feel completely alienated from society. He feels like a stranger among people, he is tormented by a sense of isolation that increases with each passing day. This anxiety becomes not only the result of his crime but also a reflection of his inner discord.

Dostoevsky masterfully conveys the protagonist's state of anxiety through his behavior, thoughts, and actions. Raskolnikov becomes paranoid, it seems to him that everyone around him knows about his crime and condemns him. He loses the ability to communicate normally, he is tormented by visions and hallucinations. Relationships with others - friends, family, even Sonya Marmeladova - become a source of pain and suffering for him, as he can no longer perceive them as he used to. This sense of alienation drives Raskolnikov to the limit, making his existence unbearable.

Raskolnikov's alienation manifests itself not only in his attitude towards others but also in his attitude towards himself. He can no longer understand his own motives; his consciousness splits apart. This leads to even more anxiety and fear that becomes an integral part of his daily life. Dostoevsky shows that the attempt to free oneself from moral obligations and to go beyond conventional norms leads to the deepest inner crisis.

(e) Meaning of Life and Death.

The questions of the meaning of life and death run through the entire novel. For Raskolnikov, these questions become especially important after he commits the murder. He begins to think about what life really means and whether it has any meaning if a man can destroy it so easily. His reflections on death become increasingly dark and disturbing.

Raskolnikov tries to find meaning in his life through the ideas of strong personalities and the right to crime, but as the plot progresses he realizes more and more that these ideas do not give him peace. He feels that he has lost something important, that his act has ruined not only the old woman's life but his own as well. This realization leads him to the idea that the real meaning of life can only be found through redemption and suffering.

For Raskolnikov, this path proves to be extremely difficult, but it is the path that leads him to spiritual rebirth. At the end of the novel, the hero begins to realize that life has value not because of power and authority, but because of love, compassion, and sincere remorse.

Albert Camus' *The Outsider*.

Albert Camus' novel *The Outsider* is one of the key works of existentialist literature in which the author explores the themes of absurdity, alienation, freedom, and responsibility through the life story of Meursault, a man who feels like an outsider in the world. Camus uses the existential method to show how Meursault faces the meaninglessness of existence and eventually comes to a certain understanding and acceptance of this absurdity.

(a) Subjective Experience

One of the central aspects of existential literature is the study of subjective experience. In The Outsider, Camus shows the inner world of the protagonist. Meursault, on whose behalf the narrative is told, is characterized by extraordinary indifference and emotional detachment. He describes the events that happen to him as if they had no meaning for him. For example, the death of his mother, which should have caused strong emotional feelings, is perceived by Meursault with indifference. He does not feel grief, and his reaction to his mother's funeral shocks others with its coldness.

This indifference manifests itself not only in his attitude to his mother's death but also in other situations in his life. Meursault does not experience joy or sadness; he lives in a world that seems to him meaningless and devoid of any purpose. His inner world reflects a deep existential crisis in which the protagonist sees no meaning in human emotions and experiences. Camus shows how the absence of any higher meaning leads a person to complete emotional devastation and indifference.

(b) Freedom and Responsibility

The themes of freedom and responsibility occupy an important place in *The Outsider*. Meursault, despite his indifference to everything that happens, realizes and accepts responsibility for his actions. In the central episode of the novel, when Meursault kills an Arab on the beach, he does not try to justify or find an explanation for his action. He simply admits that it happened. This act is devoid of any rational motive, it is done in a state of affect, under the influence of the heat and the blinding light of the sun.

Through this episode, Camus emphasizes that in a world devoid of meaning, man is still free and responsible for his actions. Freedom, according to Camus, consists in accepting the absurdity of the world and acting in spite of it. Meursault is free in his choices, but this freedom does not bring him satisfaction or happiness, it only emphasizes his alienation and loneliness. By taking responsibility for his actions, Meursault realizes his freedom, but this freedom remains a heavy and painful burden for him.

(c) Authenticity

Meursault tries to live according to his inner beliefs despite society's judgment and misunderstanding. Unlike many other characters who try to conform to society's expectations, Meursault stays true to himself. He does not try to pretend, he does not hide his true feelings and thoughts, even if they seem unacceptable to those around him.

Throughout the novel, Meursault refuses to play by the rules that society dictates to him. He does not show false emotions, nor does he strive to conform to social norms and expectations. This is evident in his behavior during the trial when, instead of defending himself and trying to justify himself, he simply acknowledges the facts, even if they are to his detriment. He realizes that his honesty and refusal to be hypocritical causes hostility and misunderstanding in society, but he continues to live according to his beliefs.

Camus shows that being honest to oneself in a world ruled by hypocrisy is a form of resistance. Meursault remains true to himself, and this loyalty gives his life a certain meaning, even if it seems meaningless to others.

(d) Anxiety and Alienation

Anxiety and alienation are the constant companions of the existential hero, and in The Outsider, Camus makes these themes central. Meursault feels alienated from society. This alienation manifests itself not only in his indifference to life but also in his inability to make genuine emotional connections with others. His relationships with others, be they friends, lovers, or casual acquaintances, lack depth and sincerity. He lives as if on the surface, not immersing himself in emotional experiences and not trying to understand the feelings of others.

The sense of alienation is especially pronounced when Meursault faces the inevitability of death. He realizes that he is truly alone in the world, that his life has no meaning, and that death is the only inevitability that awaits every human being. This thought makes him feel anxious, but also liberated at the same time. Recognizing his alienation and accepting the absurdity of existence, Meursault comes to realize that his life belongs to him alone and that he alone can give his life any meaning.

(e) Meaning of Life and Death

For Meursault, as for many existential characters, the question of the meaning of life becomes particularly acute when he faces the inevitability of death. In the final scene of the novel, as Meursault awaits the execution of his death sentence, he reflects on his life and concludes that it has been devoid of any meaning. However, this realization does not cause him despair; on the contrary, it brings him inner liberation.

Camus shows that accepting the absurdity of life and realizing one's mortality can be a source of inner freedom. Meursault realizes that there is no higher meaning or purpose in the world, that life is just an accident and death is its natural conclusion. By accepting this thought, he gains a certain peace of mind and freedom from fear. Life, according to Camus, requires no justification or explanation; its meaning lies in the very fact of existence. Man, according to Camus, can find freedom only by accepting the absurdity of his fate.

Chapter 13. Pragmatic Method

"Truth is what works."
William James "Pragmatism"

Definition:

The pragmatic method is an approach to knowledge and inquiry that is based on the principle that the truth and meaning of ideas and statements are determined by their practical implications and utility. Pragmatism emphasizes action, experience, and results, questioning abstract theories that are not proven in practice.

Landmark figures:
Charles Sanders Pierce, William James, John Dewey.

Application:

The pragmatic method is used in philosophy, psychology, education, and other social sciences to analyse and evaluate ideas and theories through the lens of their practical applicability and outcomes. In contrast to purely theoretical approaches, pragmatism focuses on how ideas work in practice, how well they help solve real-world problems, and what their consequences actually are.

This method is particularly valuable in situations where concrete solutions and effective strategies for action are needed. For example, in education, the pragmatic method is used to shape approaches to learning that aim not so much to impart abstract knowledge as to prepare students for practical tasks. In philosophy and psychology, it helps to evaluate ideas and concepts on the basis of their usefulness for human life and society, not just their internal logical consistency.

The pragmatic method allows theories to be tested through practical application, modifying them on the basis of the results and conclusions obtained. Ideas that prove their validity in practice are considered viable, while impractical theories are discarded or modified.

The Main Components of the Pragmatic Method

(a) Practical Applicability. The pragmatic method is based on the principle of practical applicability, which argues that the true value of ideas and theories is determined by their ability to solve real-world problems. Pragmatism focuses on the fact that a theory is meaningful only when it can be applied in practice and bring concrete benefits to people's lives. Ideas and statements are evaluated not only by their logical consistency or theoretical depth but primarily by their effectiveness in real-life situations.

The pragmatic approach argues that if an idea is not practical or capable of improving people's lives, its value becomes questionable. In this sense, theory is seen as a tool for achieving specific goals, whether in science, philosophy, or everyday life. Pragmatism encourages analysing each statement through the lens of its results and impact on the real world, questioning abstract concepts if they are not borne out in reality.

(b) Consequences and Results. The pragmatic method asserts that the truth of statements is determined by their consequences and results in the real world. According to pragmatism, an idea or statement must not just be logically coherent or theoretically sound, it must produce positive and useful results when put into practice. If an idea leads to an improvement in a situation or a solution to a problem, it can be considered true.

In this approach, truth is not a static and unchanging concept, as in traditional philosophy, but a dynamic and practical one. Truth is what works and what really helps people find their bearings, change, and improve the world. It is not only the theoretical aspect of an idea that is important but also its ability to affect reality and bring about concrete change. Pragmatism views truth as a process that evolves with life and evaluates it through the practical implications that an idea brings to the world.

(c) Dynamism and Adaptability. The pragmatic method emphasizes the fluidity and contextuality of knowledge, recognizing that truths and ideas are not static and eternal. In a world where conditions are constantly changing, pragmatism emphasizes the need to adapt ideas and actions to specific circumstances and situations. This means that knowledge must be flexible and evolve with the changing world.

Pragmatism rejects the notion that truths can be universal and unchanging. Instead, it argues that ideas and theories must evolve and adjust as conditions change and new challenges arise. This approach requires a willingness to abandon old methods or views when they no longer produce the expected results and to seek new approaches that are more relevant to current realities. The pragmatic method teaches that adaptability and the ability to revise one's views are key to effective action and finding relevant solutions.

(d) Experience and experimentation. The pragmatic method relies heavily on experience and **experimentation** to test and adjust ideas and theories. Theories should not remain at the level of abstract reasoning - their truth is tested through practical application. Only through empirical testing and experience can it be established whether an idea works in practice and produces real results. If a theory does not stand the test of reality, it must be either corrected or rejected.

This component emphasizes the importance of empirical verification: theories and hypotheses must be supported by real-world results. Pragmatism argues that an idea only makes sense if it is tested and proven in practical use. Logical reasoning is important, but without practical verification, it cannot be the basis for action.

(e) Interdisciplinarity. The pragmatic method strives for interdisciplinarity, bringing together knowledge and methods from different disciplines to solve complex and multilevel problems. Pragmatism recognizes that contemporary challenges cannot be solved solely within a single science or field of knowledge. An integrated and comprehensive approach requires cooperation between philosophy, science, technology, art, social science, and other disciplines.

This component emphasizes the importance of synthesizing ideas from different fields to find the best solutions. Pragmatism seeks to use a diversity of methods and perspectives to develop the most effective and practical strategies for action. In real life, many tasks - from social to scientific - require combining knowledge from different fields. This helps to gain a deeper understanding of the problem and offer more thoughtful solutions.

Pragmatic Method in the Context of Philosophy

Charles Sanders Peirce is considered the founder of pragmatism. He argued that the value of ideas is determined by their practical implications. In his view, any theory or idea should be evaluated not only by its internal logic but also by what real effects it causes in the world. In his writings, Peirce emphasized the importance of experience and experimentation in verifying the truth of claims, emphasizing that it is only through empirical confirmation that one can judge whether an idea is viable and useful.

Peirce believed that an idea in practice leads to positive results, it has meaning and value. His approach to pragmatism was the foundation for the further development of this philosophical tradition, which centers on testing ideas through their impact on reality.

William James developed the ideas of pragmatism and emphasized the practical applicability and usefulness of ideas. In his book ***Pragmatism***, he argued that the truth of statements is determined not only by their theoretical logic but also by the extent to which they are able to solve specific problems and bring benefits in real life. For James, truthfulness was a dynamic concept: if an idea helps people better orientate themselves in the world, make decisions, and achieve positive outcomes, then it can be considered true.

William James emphasized that philosophy should not be confined to abstractions, but should be useful and applicable to everyday life. His approach to pragmatism sought to make philosophical ideas of real practical use, helping people to overcome life's difficulties and find ways to a fuller and more meaningful existence.

John Dewey applied pragmatism to education and social philosophy, seeing in these fields great potential for introducing philosophical ideas that could make a difference in society. In his book ***How We Think,*** John Dewey compared thinking to a tool, like a precision instrument in the hands of a craftsman that helps solve practical problems. He emphasized the importance of experience, experimentation, and reflection as fundamental components in learning and identity formation.

For John Dewey, thinking should not remain abstract, like an idea in a void; rather, it should serve as a bridge connecting people to the real problems and challenges, they face every day. He believed that education should be based on active student participation, where learning takes place through interaction with reality, experimentation, and reflection on the results. Each student, according to John Dewey, is like an explorer who gains knowledge through action and reflection.

The central element of his philosophy was reflection - the moment when a person looks back on his actions and analyses them as if reading a map of the path he has traveled, in order to understand what to do next. It is this process that allows a person to improve and make more meaningful decisions in the future.

The pragmatic method allows us to investigate and solve specific problems by emphasizing experiences, consequences, and outcomes. In philosophy and literature, the pragmatic method helps to deepen understanding of how ideas and theories are translated into real actions and experiences, revealing their practical significance and impact.

Pragmatic Method in Literary Works

John Steinbeck's *The Grapes of Wrath*

John Steinbeck's novel *The Grapes of Wrath* is an emotionally intense work that explores the effects of the Great Depression in the United States and the migration of thousands of families forced to leave their homes in search of work and a better life. At the center of the novel is the story of the Joad family, whose lives are disrupted by economic and social changes. Steinbeck uses a pragmatic method to show how economic theories and social policies have a direct impact on the fates of people, and how these people in turn try to survive in the new environment.

An Example of the Use of the Pragmatic Method in the Book *The Grapes of Wrath*:

(a) Practical Applicability

One of the key aspects of the pragmatic method is its emphasis on the practical applicability of ideas and theories. In *The Grapes of Wrath*, Steinbeck shows how economic theories and policies implemented during the Great Depression had a direct impact on the lives of ordinary people. For example, the concept of economic efficiency and agrarian reforms that led to the mechanization of agriculture was, in theory, supposed to increase farm productivity and profitability. In practice, however, these reforms had devastating effects on families who lost their land and were displaced from their homes.

The novel illustrates how decisions made at the macroeconomic level manifest themselves in the concrete actions and experiences of people. Steinbeck emphasizes that theoretical models and policies that might seem rational and justified on paper, in real life lead to tragedies and the destruction of human lives. He shows that economic theories cannot exist in isolation from reality and must take into account the human factor, otherwise they become not just ineffective but destructive.

(b) Implications and Outcomes

Steinbeck's novel emphasizes the consequences of economic decisions and their impact on family survival. The Joads, like thousands of other migrants, face inhumane working conditions, poverty, and hunger. Steinbeck's descriptions emphasize how social structures and economic arrangements can lead to the degradation of human dignity and the destruction of family ties.

For example, one of the most tragic scenes in the novel is the description of the migrant camps, where people live in appalling conditions, deprived of any rights or opportunities to change their fate. These camps become a symbol of how a system created for economic gain leaves no room for human compassion and support. Steinbeck draws attention to the fact that social and economic structures that are supposed to improve people's lives, in fact, only exacerbate their suffering and despair.

(c) Dynamism and Adaptability

The pragmatic method also involves attention to dynamism and adaptability, and in *The Grapes of Wrath*, Steinbeck vividly shows how characters are forced to adapt to changing conditions in order to survive. The Joad family, having lost everything they had, embark on a journey west in hopes of finding work and building a new life. However, new challenges await them at every turn, requiring them to adapt to the harsh reality.

The adaptability of the characters is manifested in their readiness to change and the difficulties they face. They are forced to find new ways of survival, to change their behavior and attitude to life. Steinbeck shows that in conditions of economic instability and social injustice, those who are able to quickly adapt to new conditions survive. However, this adaptation does not always lead to a better life, and often its only result is survival on the edge of human capabilities.

(d) Experience and Experimentation

Another important aspect of the pragmatic method is the use of experience and experiment to analyse and criticize existing social and economic systems. In *The Grapes of Wrath*, Steinbeck describes the experience and experiences of his characters as a kind of experiment through which he explores the effectiveness and justice of these systems.

The experiences of the Joads and other migrants become a kind of "living experiment" that shows how the economic system works (or fails to work) in a crisis. Steinbeck uses these experiences to critically examine the existing social and economic structures that prove unable to provide for people's basic needs. The novel asks questions about how just these structures are and what needs to change to make them more humane and efficient.

Steinbeck does not simply describe the suffering of his characters. He uses their experiences as the basis for a broad social critique. He shows that real people, with their pain and suffering, cannot be reduced to numbers and statistics and that any theories and policies must come from an understanding of human experience and respect for human dignity.

Jack London's *Martin Eden*

In the novel *Martin Eden*, Jack London explores the life and aspirations of a young writer, Martin Eden, who struggles to realize his ideals and dreams in the face of harsh reality. The main character, Martin Eden, largely reflects the personal experiences of Jack London himself.

Like Martin Eden, Jack London experienced numerous difficulties on the road to literary success. Both started at the bottom and faced misunderstanding and skepticism from others before achieving recognition. Jack London put many of his own philosophical views and reflections into his character. The themes of individualism, struggle for self-assertion and self-destruction reflect the inner conflicts that the author himself faced.

An Example of the Use of the Pragmatic Method in *Martin Eden*:

(a) Practical Applicability

In *Martin Eden,* Jack London shows how the main character's personal beliefs and philosophical ideas are put to the test in real life. Martin, a young and ambitious working-class man, dreams of becoming a writer and succeeding in society. He studies philosophy, literature and self-education, forming his own views on life.

However, when the protagonist is confronted with the reality of the literary world, his ideals begin to be seriously tested. Jack London shows how Martin's beliefs pass through the filter of practical life, where they are either confirmed or disproved. For example, his belief in the power of individualism and perseverance is threatened when he realizes that success in literature depends not only on talent and work, but also on social connections, circumstance, and luck. Through this process, Jack London illustrates how theories and philosophical ideas must be applied to real life in order to have value.

(b) Implications and Outcomes

The novel *Martin Eden* also illustrates how the ideals and dreams of the protagonist affect his life and relationships with others. Martin, obsessed with the pursuit of success and self-improvement, gradually becomes alienated from the people around him. His dream of becoming a famous writer begins to destroy his personal relationships and isolate him from society. This is especially evident in his relationship with Ruth, the woman he loves and for whom he initially strives to succeed.

Jack London shows how obsession with one's ideals can lead to self-destruction. Martin achieves success, but it does not bring him satisfaction or happiness. Instead, he faces emptiness and disappointment as he realizes that his dreams and ideals, which seemed so important to him, in practice do not bring the satisfaction he expected. The results of his efforts are not what he had hoped for, with tragic consequences.

(c) Dynamism and Adaptability

Martin Eden is forced to adapt to the changing conditions of his life, which is an important aspect of the pragmatic method. Jack London describes how the hero, who started his journey from the bottom of the ladder, goes through many difficulties and obstacles to reach his goal. Martin realizes that he needs to adapt to new circumstances and change his methods in order to succeed.

For example, his attitude toward writing and the literary world changes as he faces the reality of the publishing business. He realizes that in order for his work to be accepted, he needs to change his style and approach. However, Martin also realizes that such adaptation may mean betraying his original ideals, which presents him with a difficult moral choice.

Jack London through this character shows that dynamism and the ability to adapt to change are key factors in the process of achieving goals. However, this process can also lead to the loss of one's own identity and ideals, which is what happens to Martin when he realizes that the price of his success is too high.

(d) Experience and Experimentation

Jack London uses Martin Eden's experiences and experiences to analyse and critique social and cultural norms. The entire novel can be seen as an experiment in which Martin tests his theories and beliefs in the context of real life. His journey to success and subsequent disillusionment serve as the basis for a broad critique of capitalist society and its values.

Jack London describes how Martin struggles to find his place in a society that values material success over spiritual values. Through his protagonist's experiences, Jack London criticizes the ideals of the American dream, showing that the pursuit of wealth and fame can lead to inner emptiness and alienation from oneself. Martin, who begins his journey with a sincere desire for self-improvement and learning, eventually becomes trapped by his own ambitions and social pressures.

Chapter 14. Historical-Philosophical Method

"History is a process of self-discovery of the Spirit."
Hegel's "Philosophy of History"

Definition:

The historical-philosophical method is an approach to the study and analysis of philosophical ideas and concepts in the context of their historical development. The historical-philosophical method emphasizes the historical evolution of philosophical doctrines, their influence on culture and society, and the relationship between philosophical ideas and historical events.

Landmark figures:
Georg Wilhelm Friedrich Hegel, Karl Marx, Friedrich Nietzsche.

Application:
The historical-philosophical method is used to analyse and interpret philosophical systems and concepts in the context of their historical development. This method is used to study the influence of historical events on philosophical ideas and, vice versa, the influence of philosophy on the development of society and culture.

The Main Components of the Historical-Philosophical Method

(a) Contextualization is a key component of the historical-philosophical method. This method involves considering philosophical ideas and concepts in the context of the historical events, cultural changes, and social processes that gave rise to them. Philosophical ideas do not appear suddenly, like a flash in the dark, but are always linked to the conditions of the time in which they emerged.

Contextualization allows us to penetrate deeper into the essence of philosophical doctrines, analysing how political, social, and cultural phenomena of the time influenced the formation of thoughts. It helps to see philosophical concepts not as abstract ideas, but as responses to the living challenges of the epoch. For example, Karl Marx's works cannot be fully understood without taking into account the socio-economic conditions of the 19th century, just as Immanuel Kant's ideas cannot be understood without analysing the spiritual and political realities of the Enlightenment.

This component of the historical-philosophical method makes philosophy a living response to events, helping us to understand how the ideas of the past became the foundation for the thoughts that shape our worldview today.

(b) The Historical evolution of the historical-philosophical method makes it possible to see philosophy as a living process that does not remain static but is constantly changing and adapting to new conditions and the challenges of the times. This component is similar to the study of a river that flows, changing its course but retaining its essence. Philosophical teachings go through various stages of transformation, reflection, and rethinking, which makes them more flexible and relevant in different historical contexts.

The historical-philosophical method views philosophy as a process of continuous development, in which each new generation of thinkers contributes its ideas, rethinking previous concepts and adding new nuances. This allows us to see philosophy not as a collection of fixed truths, but as a chain of ideas interconnected and evolving over time. For example, the ideas of Plato and Aristotle went through many interpretations and transformations, influencing medieval scholasticism, the Renaissance, and the Modern Age, and continue to be relevant.

Historical evolution helps us to understand why philosophical ideas that originated in the past can retain their relevance and be applicable to new realities. The evolution of philosophical doctrines is the way in which ideas are constantly reshaped and intertwined, becoming powerful intellectual tools for analysing the present.

(c) Influence and interrelationships. The historical-philosophical method emphasizes the close relationship between philosophical ideas and historical events, viewing them as two streams that intertwine and mutually influence each other. Just as wind changes the shape of trees and trees create new shadows, so philosophy influences historical developments and historical processes shape philosophical concepts. This component explores the impact of philosophical ideas on social, political, and cultural change and, in turn, how historical processes push philosophers to create new concepts.

The relationship between philosophy and history can be seen in many examples where great events became catalysts for philosophical thought. For example, the ideas of the Enlightenment had a profound impact on socio-political change in Europe in the 18th century, inspiring revolutions and reforms, while the philosophers of that era - such as Immanuel Kant and Jean-Jacques Rousseau - were in turn influenced by new scientific discoveries and societal changes. This connection emphasizes that philosophy does not exist in isolation from history, but is an active participant in it, capable of both shaping the course of events and being the result of historical change.

(d) Critical analysis, as part of the historical-philosophical method, plays the role of a compass that helps to assess the historical significance of philosophical concepts and their impact on culture and society. This component allows for a deeper understanding of which ideas have had the most powerful impact on the development of culture and thought, how they have changed social values, views on morality, politics, and science, and how they have influenced human perception of reality.

Critical analysis helps to identify the strengths and weaknesses of philosophical systems by viewing them through the lens of their real-world impact. For example, Karl Marx's philosophy not only changed the theoretical approach to economics and politics but also drove global social transformation. At the same time, critical analysis allows us to reflect on the negative effects of certain ideas, such as dogmatism or utopianism, which in their extremes could lead to destructive consequences. Critical analysis helps to separate temporary and fashionable ideas from those that have left an indelible mark on human history and to evaluate their role in creating cultural, scientific, and political paradigms.

(e) Historical reflection is a kind of mirror of time in which philosophers and historians reassess philosophical ideas, analysing how they have stood the test of time and how their meanings and perceptions have changed over the course of historical events. This component of the historical-philosophical method allows us to reflect on how ideas that once seemed immutable have been revised or modified on the basis of new historical realities and accumulated experience. Historical reflection not only assesses how relevant philosophical concepts remain but also helps to rethink them in the light of contemporary challenges.

This process of reflection allows us to take a critical look at philosophical traditions, sometimes considered axiomatic, and rethink their content. For example, the ideas of the Enlightenment, once seen as unquestionable symbols of reason and progress, were seriously criticized in the light of the historical experience of the twentieth century for their rationalism, which, as it turned out, could lead to technocracy and alienation. Reflexivity opens the door to the search for new approaches to old philosophical questions, helping to discover new solutions by drawing on the lessons of the past.

Historical-Philosophical Method in the Context of Philosophy

Georg Wilhelm Friedrich Hegel used the historical-philosophical method in his *Lectures on the History of Philosophy*. For Hegel, the history of philosophy is not simply a sequence of ideas, but a dynamic process in which each philosophical concept contributes to the development of a common understanding of being.

Hegel views the history of philosophy as the development of the absolute spirit - a process in which the spirit gradually realizes its essence, passing through various stages of development through the philosophical teachings of different epochs. This process can be visualized as a spiral movement, where each new doctrine not only reflects the achievements of the past but also raises philosophical thought to a new level. For Hegel, the philosophical ideas of antiquity, the Middle Ages, and the New Age are stages in the spirit's journey to absolute knowledge.

Georg Wilhelm Friedrich Hegel uses contextualization in his lectures, examining philosophical teachings in light of historical conditions and cultural change, as well as historical evolution, analysing how ideas have been transformed over time. Hegel sees this process as an inextricable link between philosophy and history, where the development of philosophical thought reflects the general patterns of cultural and social development.

Karl Marx applied the historical-philosophical method in Capital and The German Ideology, analysing the development of socio-economic formations and the role of philosophical ideas in the historical process. Karl Marx viewed philosophy not in isolation from material conditions but as part of a broader context - the historical development of society. He emphasized that philosophical ideas always reflect the economic and social realities of their time.

Karl Marx viewed history as a process of class struggle and the development of productive forces. This view of history allowed him to analyse how the change in economic systems - from slave to feudal, from feudal to capitalist - was accompanied by changes in philosophical and ideological concepts. Karl Marx used contextualization to show how the ideas of philosophers such as John Locke or Jean-Jacques Rousseau emerged in the context of social transformations and the struggle for new forms of production and distribution.

Karl Marx emphasized that the development of productive forces and changes in property relations lead to a change in social formations. This leads to the transformation not only of economic structures, but also of philosophical views, which emerge as an ideological reflection of these material changes.

Friedrich Nietzsche used the historical-philosophical method in *Thus Spoke Zarathustra* and *The Genealogy of Morals*, in which he explored how moral and cultural values develop and change under the influence of philosophical ideas and historical events. Nietzsche looked at morality as something unstable and changeable, evolving according to time and culture, rather than as an unchanging truth. He criticized traditional values such as Christian morality and European cultural norms, seeing in them traces of weakness and suppression of the will.

In ***The Genealogy of Morality***, Friedrich Nietzsche applies critical analysis to understand how moral concepts such as good and evil have been formed historically and how they have been used to subjugate and control people. He views morality not as an eternal truth, but as a historically conditioned system of views that serve the interests of certain groups. This reassessment of moral values through historical reflection allows Nietzsche to conceptualize traditional moral principles in terms of their strength and weakness.

In ***Thus Spoke Zarathustra***, Nietzsche uses the historical-philosophical method to create the image of superman, a man who discards outdated moral norms and creates new values corresponding to his inner strength and will to live. Through this image, he shows how the development of cultural values must take place through constant rethinking and overcoming of the past, which makes his ideas relevant in the context of modern historical development.

Historical-Philosophical Methods in Literary Works

Leo Tolstoy's novel ***War and Peace*** is one of the greatest works of world literature, in which the author combines historical and philosophical analysis. Leo Tolstoy uses the historical-philosophical method to show how historical events are intertwined with the personal destinies of his characters and also reflects deeply on the nature of war, peace, and human existence.

(a) Contextualization

One of the key elements of the historical and philosophical method in *War and Peace* is contextualization, through which Leo Tolstoy immerses the reader in the era of the War of 1812. The author does not just describe the events but also shows how they are reflected in the lives of his characters. At the center of the narrative are the Bolkonsky, Rostov, and Bezukhov families, whose fates are closely connected with historical events. Leo Tolstoy shows how the war changes the lives of these people, forces them to reconsider their views and values, and confronts them with new, sometimes tragic, circumstances.

For example, Duke Andrei Bolkonsky, one of the main characters of the novel, at the beginning of the narrative aspires to glory and sees war as a way to realize his ambitions. However, faced with the reality of war, he gradually realizes its horror and senselessness, which leads him to profound internal changes. Leo Tolstoy through the fate of Andrei Bolkonsky and other characters shows how war not only destroys physically but also has a powerful effect on the spiritual world of a person, forcing him to rethink his values and goals in life.

(b) Historical Evolution

War and Peace is a study of historical evolution - both of individuals and of society as a whole. Leo Tolstoy describes in detail how war changes social structures, political institutions, and public sentiment.

For example, Natasha Rostova goes through the difficult process of growing up, facing the hardships and tragedies of war. Her naive and romantic nature is put to the test, and she gradually becomes more mature and conscious. Similar changes occur with other characters who are forced to adapt to new conditions.

Leo Tolstoy also explores broader historical processes, such as the fall and recovery of the national spirit, changes in relations between different social strata, and the political consequences of war. He shows how historical events lead to the evolution of society, changing its structure and values.

(c) Influence and Interrelationships

Leo Tolstoy analyses the relationship between historical events and personal destinies. In War and Peace, history does not act as a backdrop to the characters' lives but is an integral part of their destinies. Leo Tolstoy shows how the actions of individuals can influence the course of history, but also emphasizes that people's fates are often subject to forces they cannot control.

For example, Leo Tolstoy explores the theme of fate and free will through the character of Pierre Bezukhov, who becomes involved in war and political intrigue. Despite his attempts to find meaning and purpose in life, Pierre is confronted by forces that are much stronger than himself. Leo Tolstoy shows that historical events, such as war, often prove to be decisive factors in determining people's fates, and that these events are not always under human control.

(d) Critical Analysis

One important aspect of the historical-philosophical method in the novel *War and Peace* is the critical analysis of war and its impact on human nature and society. Leo Tolstoy does not simply describe military action but reflects on the nature of war, its causes, and consequences. He is critical of the glorification of war and shows it as an integral part of human history.

Leo Tolstoy views war as a manifestation of destructive forces that lead to the suffering and death of many people. He shows that war is often driven by ambition, personal interests, and political games and that its consequences are always tragic. The author also explores the theme of the moral responsibility of leaders and commanders whose decisions affect the fates of millions of people. Through his characters, Leo Tolstoy expresses doubts that war can be justified or that it can lead to any positive results.

(e) Historical Reflection

Leo Tolstoy deeply reflects on historical events, considering them from a philosophical point of view. In *War and Peace,* he not only describes the war but also reflects on its meaning, and tries to understand why it happens and what lessons can be learned from it. Leo Tolstoy asks questions about the meaning of history, the role of the individual in history, and how human actions relate to broader historical processes.

For example, Leo Tolstoy, in his reflections, often comes to the idea that history is driven not so much by the efforts of individual personalities, but by deeper, hidden forces that cannot always be realized or understood. He argues that war and peace are not simply opposing states, but are complex and interrelated processes that must be seen in the context of all of human history.

Leo Tolstoy also reflects on the role of chance in history, showing how sometimes insignificant events can lead to huge consequences. In this context, he criticizes the traditional understanding of history as the result of the actions of great men, offering a more complex and multi-layered understanding of the historical process.

Chapter 15. Dialogical Method

"Truth is born in dialogue."
Mikhail Bakhtin's "Problems of Dostoevsky's Poetics"

Definition:

The dialogical method is an approach to research and analysis that is based on a dialogue between different perspectives, arguments, and contexts. The dialogical method emphasizes interaction, mutual understanding, and exchange of ideas between the participants in the dialogue, which contributes to a deeper understanding and enriched knowledge.

Landmark figures:
Socrates, Mikhail Bakhtin, Hans-Georg Gadamer.

Application:
The dialogical method is used in philosophy, literature, psychology, and pedagogy to analyse and understand complex issues through dialogue and interaction between different points of view. This method is used to identify and explore contradictions, find compromises, and enrich knowledge through the exchange of ideas.

The Main Components of the Dialogical Method

a) Interaction is a key element of the dialogical method, based on an active exchange of ideas and arguments between participants. Dialogue is not simply a transfer of information, but a lively collaboration where the thoughts and attitudes of each participant influence the course of the conversation.

Interaction in this context is like a dance - each party takes into account the movements of the other, striving for harmony and understanding.

An open and honest exchange of ideas encourages each participant not only to express his or her ideas but also to listen to the other's point of view, enriching the common vision of the issue. It is important not just to defend one's position, but also to accept the thoughts of the interlocutor as an equal contribution. This creates a space for a joint search for truth and solving complex problems. The dialogic method turns the discussion into a process in which truth is shaped through interaction and mutual influence.

(b) Diversity of perspectives is a fundamental component of the dialogical method, which allows for the inclusion of different views and contexts. Just as light is refracted through the many facets of a crystal, each new perspective reveals different aspects of the same problem, allowing it to be examined in a deeper and more multifaceted way. The dialogical method recognizes that truth is rarely simple and that its attainment requires consideration of different cultural, philosophical, and personal aspects.

Dialogue becomes a space to include and compare different views, which makes it possible not only to see a problem from different angles but also to find more integrated and comprehensive solutions. Recognizing diversity not only enriches the communication process itself but also helps to find solutions that would not be possible without the exchange of different views. Such an approach fosters a deeper understanding of issues where each perspective becomes part of a single constructive analysis.

(c) Mutual understanding is one of the main objectives of the dialogical method, like a bridge that connects different shores, making it possible for ideas and points of view to meet. Dialogue does not seek to make one side win by suppressing the other - rather, it seeks to reconcile differences through open discussion and compromise.

The process of dialogue is like carefully tuning a musical instrument, where each opinion is a string that needs to be heard and tuned in harmony with others. Mutual understanding helps participants gain a deeper insight into each other's positions, which in turn helps them find common ground and create a fruitful, constructive dialogue. Instead of a struggle for supremacy, the dialogic method helps build a collaborative space where every idea matters and contributes to a shared understanding of the problem.

(d) Critical examination is a key element of the dialogical method, which turns the exchange of views into a process of in-depth analysis and verification. Just as a jeweler examines a precious stone for flaws, participants in a dialogue do not simply take statements on faith, but carefully analyse them, checking the logic of the argument and identifying possible weaknesses.

This component helps to avoid superficial judgments and makes the discussion more meaningful and productive. It is important not to reject an idea at once, but to examine it for its strength, subjecting it to close scrutiny and revealing hidden aspects. A critical approach in dialogue does not destroy communication, but on the contrary, it helps to clear it of unchecked judgments and hasty conclusions, which leads to a deeper understanding and a qualitative solution to the issues under discussion.

e) **Knowledge enrichment** is one of the most valuable aspects of the dialogical method. Dialogue is like a river which, by absorbing the waters of different sources, becomes more and more abundant. Through interaction and exchange, participants broaden their horizons, learn new aspects of the issues under discussion, and even revise their own views. Dialogue not only helps to reveal hidden sides of issues but also becomes a powerful tool for learning and development.

Each participant brings his or her own unique experience to the dialogue, which becomes the basis for discovering truth together. Sharing knowledge enriches everyone, making the discussion not just a process of asserting one's point of view, but a shared journey of discovery.

The Dialogical Method in the Context of Philosophy

Socrates is one of the founders of the dialogical method, and his contribution to the development of this philosophical tradition remains fundamental. In Plato's dialogues, Socrates utilizes the method of maieutics - or Socratic dialogue - which is based on questions and answers. This method can be compared to the art of midwifery, where Socrates, like a wise mentor, helps his interlocutors to "give birth" to the truth on their own, without imposing ready-made answers on them.

Socrates did not seek to be a teacher in the traditional sense of imparting knowledge; his goal was to encourage his interlocutors to search for truth on their own. He asked leading questions, forcing them to think, question their own beliefs, and search for a logical basis for their assertions. In this way, dialogue became not just a way of transmitting information, but a path to self-discovery and deeper understanding.

Plato, through the mouth of Socrates, emphasized the importance of dialogue as a method of searching for truth and substantiation of knowledge. Dialogue became a way of not just exchanging opinions, but a means of clarifying thoughts, finding weaknesses in arguments and, ultimately, approaching a more complete and objective understanding.

Mikhail Bakhtin developed the ideas of dialogueism in his works on literary theory and philosophy of language, emphasizing that dialogicality is a fundamental characteristic of both language and culture as a whole. Bakhtin argued that any utterance or text never exists in isolation, like a lone note in a symphony; on the contrary, every utterance is in constant dialogic interaction with other utterances, ideas, and texts.

For Bakhtin, language is not just a means of transmitting information, but a field for interaction, where the voices of different participants, their thoughts, and opinions intertwine and influence each other. In this context, each text or utterance becomes a response to the previous ones and, at the same time, an expectation of the next. Dialogicality permeates everything - from everyday speech to cultural phenomena, and culture as a whole is seen as an open dialogue in which there is no single correct voice, but many different points of view and interpretations.

Bakhtin's concept of dialogism shows that every text carries echoes of other texts, and any new utterance always takes into account and reinterprets those that have been said before.

Hans-Georg Gadamer in *Truth and Method* developed the ideas of hermeneutic dialogue, emphasizing that the process of understanding texts and cultural phenomena always occurs through dialogue and interaction between the interpreter and the text. Gadamer argued that understanding is not a one-way act where the reader simply receives information from the text; on the contrary, it is a meeting of two worlds - the world of the interpreter and the world of the text, which resembles a conversation in which both participants enrich each other.

For Gadamer, the dialogue between the interpreter and the text is a living process in which one comes into contact with the cultural heritage, traditions, and meanings hidden in the text. He emphasized that historical and cultural contexts are important for proper understanding and that the interpreter always brings his or her own anticipations and expectations to the process, which makes understanding dynamic and evolving. The text seems to "respond" to these expectations by opening up new horizons of meaning.

Gadamer believed that true understanding is impossible without this dialogical interaction, in which the interpreter does not just passively perceive the text, but actively participates in the creation of meaning. Through such hermeneutic dialogue, cultural phenomena and texts take on new life and relevance, each time rediscovering themselves in the process of interaction with the person reading them.

The Dialogic Method in Literary Works

In ***The Brothers Karamazov*, Fyodor Dostoevsky** uses the dialogic method to explore complex philosophical, moral, and religious issues. Dialogues between characters play a central role in the novel, allowing Dostoevsky to show the diversity of viewpoints and the depth of human experience.

(a) Interaction

One of the key aspects of the dialogic method in the novel is the interaction between the characters, especially between the Karamazov brothers. Dostoevsky shows how their dialogues become an arena for the discussion of important philosophical and moral issues. Ivan, Alexei (Alyosha), and Dmitri Karamazov represent different life positions and views of the world. Their interaction allows us to explore these differences.

For example, in the famous scene of The Grand Inquisitor, Ivan Karamazov sets forth his doubts about divine justice and the meaning of faith, while Alyosha, a more religious and spiritual character, seeks to understand and answer these doubts. The dialogue between the two reveals not only the conflict of their worldviews, but also the larger theme of human suffering, freedom, and faith.

(b) Diversity of Perspectives

The Brothers Karamazov is a novel that presents many different points of view and philosophical positions. Dostoevsky introduces different characters into the narrative, each representing a unique position. For example, Ivan Karamazov represents a rationalistic and nihilistic approach, while Alyosha represents a religious and spiritual path. Dmitri represents the passionate and sensual side of human nature.

The dialogues between these characters allow the reader to see different aspects of the same issue, which contributes to deep analysis and understanding of complex themes. The diversity of viewpoints in the novel allows Dostoevsky to explore questions of faith, morality, free will, justice, and human nature from different angles, not offering unambiguous answers, but encouraging the reader to reflect on these questions for himself.

(c) Mutual Understanding

Dialogues in *The Brothers Karamazov* serve as a means of achieving mutual understanding between the characters.

Despite their differing views and beliefs, the characters in the novel seek dialogue in order to understand each other and resolve their internal and external conflicts. For example, the relationship between Ivan and Alyosha, despite their differences, is based on attempts to understand and accept the other's point of view.

Dostoevsky shows that dialogue can be a way not only to express one's thoughts but also to come to some common understanding, even if complete agreement is unattainable. The characters in the novel not only discuss philosophical issues through dialogue but also strive for personal understanding, which makes the dialogue in the novel even more profound and multilayered.

(d) Critical examination

The dialogical method allows Dostoevsky to critically analyse the ideas and arguments presented by the characters. Through dialogues, he questions various philosophical positions and moral principles, exploring their internal contradictions and weaknesses. For example, the dialogues between Ivan and Alyosha explore the issue of divine justice and the suffering of children, where Ivan expresses his indignation and doubt in the existence of a just God, and Alyosha tries to find an answer to this challenge based on faith and love.

Dostoevsky does not give direct answers to the questions posed, but through the dialogical method allows the reader to see how different ideas can come into conflict and be critically analysed.

(e) Knowledge Enrichment

Dialogues in the novel contribute to enriching the knowledge of both characters and readers. Through dialogues,

Dostoevsky introduces complex philosophical and religious ideas into the narrative, making them available for deeper reflection. For example, Ivan's dialogue with the Devil in the chapter "Rebellion" allows him to express his doubts and fears, as well as explore the idea of moral relativism and nihilism.

Dialogues not only deepen the reader's understanding of philosophical and moral issues but also enrich the inner world of the characters themselves. The characters grow and develop in the process of dialogue, encountering new ideas and having to rethink their beliefs. This makes Dostoevsky's novel not just an account of events, but a profound exploration of the human soul and its possibilities.

Herman Hesse, *The Bead Game.*

Herman Hesse, winner of the Nobel Prize for Literature, worked on the novel *The Bead Game* for eleven years. It is his last major novel and was published in 1943. In this profound and multi-layered work, Hermann Hesse explores the dialogue between different cultural and intellectual traditions through the symbolic game of beads. This unusual game epitomizes the interaction and exchange of ideas, presenting an exquisite interweaving of thoughts and concepts that reflects humanity's quest for knowledge and harmony.

(a) Interaction

In *The Bead Game*, Hesse shows the dialogue and interaction between different cultural and intellectual traditions through a mysterious game of beads. The bead game is a metaphor for a complex and multilayered dialogue in which the participants, members of the Castalian elite, synthesize ideas from different fields of knowledge: music, mathematics, philosophy, and art.

The protagonist, Joseph Knecht interacts with these traditions in an effort to understand and integrate them into a harmonious whole. Hesse uses interaction in play as a way of showing how different cultural and intellectual heritages can enrich each other and create new meanings. This dialogue is not limited to formal play; it is also evident in the relationships between the characters, their conversations, and reflections, during which they discuss and compare different traditions and ideas.

(b) Diversity of Perspectives

The Bead Game incorporates many different cultural and intellectual traditions, allowing Hesse to deeply analyse and understand complex issues. The novel presents ideas from Western and Eastern philosophy, science, art, religion, and other areas of knowledge. These diverse traditions and perspectives intersect and interact in a bead game in which each idea or symbol becomes part of a larger intellectual picture.

Hesse shows that a diversity of perspectives contributes to a deeper understanding and synthesis of knowledge. For example, a game can incorporate elements from Bach's music, mathematical formulas, or Plato's philosophy while creating new meaning and significance. This diversity emphasizes the importance of openness to different traditions and ideas, and a willingness to dialogue and collaborate among them.

(c) Mutual Understanding

One important aspect of the dialogic method in the novel is the characters' desire for mutual understanding and synthesis of different traditions and ideas through dialogue. The bead game becomes a tool for achieving this mutual understanding, where the participants strive to combine disparate elements into a harmonious and meaningful whole.

Josef Knecht and the other participants of the game strive not just to mechanically combine different elements, but to deeply understand their essence and significance. This desire for mutual understanding is manifested in the dialogues and reflections of the characters, in which they discuss the nature of the game, its purpose and meaning, and its role in the preservation and development of cultural traditions.

(d) Critical Examination

Hermann Hesse uses the symbolic bead game to critically analyse and synthesize different ideas and traditions. The bead game allows participants not only to bring ideas together, but also to think critically about them, to see their weaknesses and strengths, and to evaluate their significance in the context of a shared intellectual culture.

Through his characters and the structure of the game itself, Hesse shows that true understanding and synthesis require a critical approach and the ability to question established notions. For example, Knecht, reflecting on the game, comes to the realization that the closed nature of the Castalian system may be an obstacle to its further development. He seeks to find a balance between tradition and innovation.

(e) Knowledge Enrichment

Dialogue and interaction in the novel contribute to the enrichment of knowledge and the deepening of understanding of cultural and intellectual traditions. Hesse shows that through play and dialogue, the participants can not only preserve and transmit accumulated knowledge but also open new horizons, expanding intellectual and spiritual possibilities.

The bead game shows that knowledge is not a static quantity, but is constantly evolving and enriched through the interaction of different cultures and traditions.

The dialogical method allows for the critical examination of various topics and the exploration and enrichment of knowledge through the exchange of ideas and mutual understanding between people engaged in dialogue. In philosophy and literature, the dialogical method helps to deepen understanding of the interaction and mutual influence of different ideas and traditions, revealing their significance for cultural and intellectual development.

Chapter 16. Deconstructivist Method

"There is nothing outside the text."
Jacques Derrida's "On Grammatology"

Definition:

The deconstructivist method is an approach to analysing and interpreting texts and cultural phenomena that seeks to identify and critique hidden assumptions, contradictions, and instability in structures of meaning.

The deconstructivist method is based on the idea that texts and meanings are not fixed and unambiguous, but are subject to multiple interpretations and constant revision.

Landmark figures:
Jacques Derrida, Paul de Man

Application:
The deconstructivist method is used in literary criticism, philosophy, cultural studies, and other humanities to analyse texts, linguistic structures, and cultural phenomena in depth. This method seeks to identify and criticize hidden assumptions, contradictions, and instabilities in structures of meaning that often go unnoticed in a traditional approach to a text or phenomenon. Deconstructivism shows that the apparent clarity and structure of a text can hide subtle internal tensions and contradictions that undermine its integrity.

The aim of the deconstructivist method is to expose these hidden internal conflicts and demonstrate how texts or concepts deconstruct themselves through their own unconscious assumptions. This method allows us to rethink traditional ideas and categories by criticizing them and revealing their relativity and conventionality. In this way, deconstructivism not only destroys familiar structures but also opens up the possibility for a new reading and re-evaluation of ideas.

In literature and philosophy, deconstructivism is used to investigate language in which meanings are constantly changing depending on context, and how every attempt to give a text a definite meaning inevitably gives rise to multiple interpretations and ambiguities.

The Main Components of the Deconstructivist Method

a) Unmasking is a key component of the deconstructivist method, which focuses on revealing hidden assumptions, contradictions, and instabilities in texts and structures of meaning. In this process, deconstructivism seeks to show that texts, ideas, or cultural structures are not as unambiguous as they may appear at first glance. The apparent logic and structure of a text often hide unresolved internal conflicts, ambiguities, or paradoxes that destroy its integrity.

This component aims to reveal hidden elements, such as unconscious biases, inconsistencies between external meaning and internal logic, or unstable boundaries between oppositions (e.g., reason and feeling, truth, and falsehood). Unmasking helps to show how these contradictions and subtexts affect our perception of a text and its interpretation, suggesting many possible meanings rather than the only correct one. It allows us to reconsider and question meanings that were previously perceived as unquestionable.

(b) Deconstruction is a process in which a text is taken apart in order to reveal its multiple interpretations and instability. Unlike traditional analysis, which seeks to find a single and complete interpretation, deconstruction destroys the illusion of coherence and completeness of meaning. It shows that any text or idea is open to multiple interpretations, which may contradict each other or be mutually exclusive.

Deconstruction emphasizes the fragmentation and multi-layering of meanings, which intertwine and overlap, creating complex networks of interpretations. It resembles a process of peeling away one layer after another, where each new meaning reveals another, potentially conflicting with the previous one. Deconstruction emphasizes that any attempt to "reassemble" a text into one whole will always lead to unstable results since every text by its very nature contains contradictions, ambiguities, and openness to revision.

This approach helps to demonstrate that meanings are not fixed, but are revised and changed depending on context, cultural assumptions, and the reader's perception. As a result, deconstruction opens up the possibility for a freer and more flexible approach to texts and ideas where there is no single correct interpretation.

(c) Critical Rethinking in the deconstructivist method consists in criticizing and revising traditional concepts, categories, and binary oppositions such as "good and evil", "truth and falsehood", "light and darkness". This component seeks to blur the strict boundaries between opposites, demonstrating that these dichotomies are often artificial constructs that do not reflect the true complexity and diversity of reality.

Deconstruction seeks to show that such binary oppositions can be superficial and reduce reality to a black and white perception, ignoring the intermediate states, paradoxes, and intertwining meanings that are always present in language, culture, and thought. Rethinking these categories allows us to see that each side of the dichotomy can hide an element of the other and that the boundaries between them are fluid and relative.

This rethinking opens up the possibility of creating new ways of understanding and interpreting texts and phenomena that go beyond the usual binary oppositions. This destruction of old categories not only critiques traditional views but also offers new avenues for analysis, recognizing the complexity and multilayered nature of the world that cannot be simply divided into opposites.

(d) Intertextuality in the deconstructivist method focuses on the interrelationships between texts, their influence on each other, and the change of meanings according to context and intersecting meanings. Deconstruction sees the text as part of a wider network of texts and ideas, where each new text inevitably interacts with others, absorbing their elements or referring to them.

Just as a river cannot exist without tributaries, no text exists in isolation. It is woven into a complex system of references, allusions, and quotations, where meanings constantly flow from one text to another, transforming and opening up new facets. Deconstruction explores how one text can reinterpret, undermine, or complement the meaning of another, and how textual overlaps create multiple interpretations.

Intertextuality emphasizes that the meaning of a text is always contextual and cannot be understood outside of its relationship to other works, ideas, and cultural phenomena. This component reveals hidden references, cultural codes, and literary allusions that enrich the text and make it multilayered.

e) Polyphony is the recognition of multiple interpretations and meanings and the rejection of the idea of a single correct interpretation of a text or concept. This component emphasizes that there is no one final truth or one correct answer, and each text is revealed in a new way depending on context, perception, and reading experience.

Just as musical polyphony is created from the combination of different melodies that interact to form a harmonious whole, so in deconstruction different interpretations exist simultaneously, interacting and creating new meanings. Polyphony allows us to look at a text or idea from different angles, where each "voice" has its own value, and no interpretation can be definitively rejected or recognized as the only correct one.

This approach opens the door to free and multifaceted interpretation, where multiple perspectives and voices coexist, enriching the understanding of the text. Polyphony in deconstruction becomes not only a tool for destroying sole truths but also a method for creating a space in which each interpretation can be heard and considered.

The Deconstructivist Method in the Context of Philosophy

Jacques Derrida, the founder of deconstruction, in ***On Grammatology*** and ***Writing and Difference***, analyses and critiques traditional notions of language, writing, and meaning. Derrida shows that meanings in texts are not stable and fixed; rather, they are subject to multiple interpretations and constant revision.

He emphasizes that language and writing are not simply means of conveying meaning, but complex structures that themselves carry instability and ambiguity. In his works,

Derrida explores how texts are always open to different interpretations that depend on the context and the reader's perception. In the process of reading, Derrida argues, meaning is not only created but also destroyed, opening up a multitude of new interpretations.

Deconstruction in Derrida's understanding aims at breaking the illusion of a single and absolute meaning, showing that every text is a field of play of meanings, where each element can change its significance depending on the reader's perspective or cultural context.

Paul de Man developed the ideas of deconstruction in literary criticism, analysing and critiquing traditional notions of literature and meaning. In his work, *Allegories of Reading*, Paul de Man shows that texts and meanings have a plurality of interpretations and often contain internal contradictions that undermine their apparent integrity.

De Man argues that any text is not a transparent or obvious carrier of meaning, as traditional criticism tends to assume. Rather, each text is a scene of complex interactions between different layers of meaning, which may be allegorical, metaphorical, or ironic. These layers of meaning are often in conflict with each other, generating instability and ambiguity, and leaving the text open to many different interpretations.

An Example of the Use of the Deconstructivist Method in Literary Works
William Shakespeare, *Hamlet*

In this work, Shakespeare creates complex linguistic structures and multi-layered characters, making it an ideal subject for deconstructivist analysis.

(a) Disclosure

When we talk about the deconstructivist analysis of *Hamlet*, we mean applying the deconstructivist method to the analysis of Shakespeare's play to show how different interpretations and readings can change the understanding of the plot and characters. In *Hamlet*, Shakespeare shows that the motivations and actions of the characters are often full of internal contradictions. Hamlet is a complex and contradictory character: he is both determined and indecisive, filled with the desire to avenge his father's murder, but constantly doubts the legitimacy of his actions. These contradictions make his character unstable, causing the audience to question his true intentions and motivations.

In addition, the behavior of other characters such as Claudius, Gertrude, and Ophelia is also ambiguous. Their motives are not always clear, which creates additional tension and complicates understanding of the plot. Shakespeare demonstrates that none of the characters are completely "right" or "wrong", showing the multi-layered and unstable nature of human nature.

(b) Deconstruction

A deconstructivist analysis of *Hamlet* allows us to consider how different interpretations and readings of the text can change our understanding of the plot and characters. For example, Hamlet's monologue 'To be or not to be' can be interpreted in different ways depending on what emphases are placed in the interpretation: is he contemplating suicide, the meaning of life, action, and inaction, or do we see the character in doubt and unable to make a choice? Different readings of this scene can radically change the perception of the entire work.

Shakespeare leaves the text open to multiple interpretations, which makes it an ideal object for deconstruction. Each act and each remark can be examined from different perspectives, allowing for a new understanding of the characters and their motivations. Deconstructivism here helps to reveal that there is no single correct answer to the questions Shakespeare poses to us.

(c) Critical rethinking
Shakespeare in *Hamlet* revises traditional notions of revenge, power, and moral dilemmas by offering multiple perspectives. The question of revenge, which is at the heart of the plot, is questioned by Hamlet himself. He constantly ponders the validity of his desire to avenge his father's death, which leads to a multitude of moral and philosophical questions. Shakespeare does not give an unambiguous answer to these questions, leaving the audience in a state of uncertainty.

Traditional notions of power and moral values are also critically reinterpreted. Claudius, who usurped the throne, is not portrayed as an unambiguously evil character; his motives and actions can be interpreted in different ways.

(d) Intertextuality
Hamlet is rich in intertextual references that make it an ideal subject for deconstructivist analysis. Shakespeare includes references to other literary and cultural works in the text, such as ancient Greek myths, Christian symbolism, and medieval literature. These references create a multi-layered text and allow the text to be analysed in the context of a broader cultural field.

For example, the comparison of Hamlet to Hercules or references to the story of Cain and Abel emphasize the complex relationships between the characters and their struggle with their own inner demons. These intertextual elements allow Hamlet to be seen as part of a larger cultural and philosophical discourse, making multiple readings and interpretations possible.

(e) Polyphony
Hamlet includes multiple points of view, which emphasizes the complexity and multi-layered nature of the text. Shakespeare creates a polyphonic structure where each character has a unique perspective on what is happening. This polyphony allows various philosophical and moral issues to intersect and dialogue with each other.

Hamlet, Claudius, Gertrude, Polonius, Ophelia, and other characters represent different views on power, love, morality, life, and death. Their dialogues and monologues create a multi-layered narrative where every word and gesture can be interpreted in different ways. This polyphony emphasizes that there is no one dominant point of view in Hamlet, and the text remains open to multiple readings and interpretations.

Franz Kafka, *The Transfiguration*
Franz Kafka's novel *The Transfiguration* is a vivid example of a text that can be analysed using the deconstructivist method. Kafka creates an absurd and multilayered reality where the boundaries between normal and abnormal, human and non-human, personal and social become blurred. Let us consider how the main aspects of deconstructivism manifest themselves in this work.

An Example of the Use of the Deconstructivist Method in *The Transfiguration*:

(a) Disclosure

One of the key elements of deconstructivist analysis in *The Transfiguration* is the exposure of hidden assumptions and contradictions in the perception and attitude towards Gregor Zamza after his transformation into a giant insect. Kafka shows how the change in Gregor's appearance radically alters the attitude of his family and society as a whole towards him. At first, when Gregor was a human being and provided for the family, he was seen as a necessary and important member of the family. However, after his transformation, his attitude towards him changes drastically - he begins to be seen as a burden and a threat.

This change demonstrates the internal contradictions in the perceptions of human value and identity. Kafka exposes the conventionality of these perceptions by showing that perceptions and attitudes towards a person can change dramatically if their outward appearance falls outside of accepted norms. Gregor's transformation becomes a metaphor for exposing how society and family build their relationships based on external, superficial characteristics.

(b) Deconstruction

The deconstructivist analysis of *The Transfiguration* reveals multiple interpretations and understandings of Gregor's metamorphosis and its symbolic meaning. Gregor's transformation into an insect can be seen from different perspectives: as a symbol of alienation, loss of identity, crisis of family relationships, or even as a metaphor for mental or physical illness.

Each of these interpretations reveals different aspects of the work and its symbolism. For example, Gregor's transformation can be seen as an expression of his inner sense of alienation and inability to conform to the expectations of his family and society. The deconstructivist approach allows all these interpretations to be seen as equal and complementary rather than mutually exclusive. This creates a multi-layered understanding of the text, where there is no one "right" answer to the question of the meaning of metamorphosis.

(c) Critical rethinking

Kafka, in The Transfiguration, revises traditional notions of human identity, normality, and family. Gregor's transformation challenges the fundamental notions of what it means to be human. His family, instead of supporting him, rejects him. It forces the reader to consider the nature of family ties and how much they are conditioned by social norms and expectations.

Kafka criticizes the notion of normality, showing that the "abnormal" in the perception of society can only be the result of a superficial and shallow approach to understanding human nature. Gregor's family, considering his existence after his transformation useless and shameful, symbolizes a society that rejects everything that does not fit into its rigid framework.

(d) Intertextuality

Kafka's work is saturated with cultural and literary references. This makes it a rich object for intertextual analysis. In *The Transfiguration*, one can find references to myths, religious texts, and literary traditions. For example, Gregor's transformation can be associated with mythology, where transformations often symbolize transitions between different states of being or consciousness.

Intertextual elements can also be found in the descriptions of family and social roles that echo the traditions of realist literature but in a twisted and absurd form. These references create additional layers of meaning and allow The Transfiguration to be seen as part of a broader cultural context, which in turn opens up new possibilities for interpretation and analysis.

(e) Polyphony

The Transfiguration incorporates different perspectives and interpretations, emphasizing the complexity and multi-layered nature of the text. Although the narrative is in the third person, Gregor's inner world, his thoughts and feelings are presented in detail, creating a multi-voiced perception of what is happening. We see how Gregor makes sense of his new condition, how his family reacts to it, and how these different points of view intersect and conflict.

The polyphony of the text is also evident in the fact that each of these viewpoints is not definitive or dominant. Kafka creates the text where all voices are equal and none of them can claim to fully understand or explain what is happening. This creates an openness to the text and leaves its interpretation up to the reader, which is one of the key features of deconstructivist analysis.

INSTEAD OF CONCLUSION

Knowledge of philosophical methods helps to navigate the chaos of everyday life, opens new horizons of understanding, and gives clarity to what seems confusing and incomprehensible. Questions about the meaning of life, about values, about freedom, and responsibility inevitably arise in every person's life. Philosophical methods help you find answers to all these questions. They give you the opportunity to build your own picture of the world and find a way out of situations that seem hopeless to others. Using them, you will learn to think for yourself, avoiding templates and clichés imposed on you. Whether you are a scientist, engineer, artist, or entrepreneur by profession, philosophical methods will make your thinking lively and malleable, allowing you to see the whole picture where others see only fragmented pieces of the mosaic.

Every method covered in this book is a tool for understanding how the world works and how we can exist in it. It is an invaluable skill for anyone who seeks to make well-argued decisions, whether in politics, business, science, or personal relationships.

Literature

1. **Aristotle** (1999). *Nicomachean Ethics.* Trans. Terence Irwin. Indianapolis: Hackett Publishing.
2. **Camus, Albert** (1989). *The Stranger.* Trans. Matthew Ward. New York: Vintage International.
3. **Camus, Albert** (1991). *The Plague.* Trans. Stuart Gilbert. New York: Vintage International.
4. **Descartes, René** (1993). *Meditations on First Philosophy.* Trans. Donald A. Cress. Indianapolis: Hackett Publishing.
5. **Dostoevsky, Fyodor** (2014). *Crime and Punishment.* Trans. Oliver Ready. New York: Penguin.
6. **Eco, Umberto** (1983). *The Name of the Rose.* Trans. William Weaver. New York: Mariner Books.
7. **Feyerabend, Paul** (1975). *Against Method.* London: Verso.
8. **Gadamer, Hans-Georg** (2004). *Truth and Method.* Trans. Joel Weinsheimer and Donald G. Marshall. London: Bloomsbury.
9. **García Márquez, Gabriel** (2006). *One Hundred Years of Solitude.* Trans. Gregory Rabassa. New York: Harper Perennial.
10. **Goethe, Johann Wolfgang von** (1962). *Faust.* Trans. Walter Kaufmann. New York: Anchor Books.
11. **Hegel, Georg Wilhelm Friedrich** (1977). *Phenomenology of Spirit.* Trans. A. V. Miller. Oxford: Oxford University Press.
12. **Heidegger, Martin** (1962). *Being and Time.* Trans. John Macquarrie and Edward Robinson. New York: Harper & Row.
13. **Hesse, Hermann** (2002). *The Glass Bead Game.* Trans. Richard and Clara Winston. New York: Picador.
14. **Kafka, Franz** (1998). *The Trial.* Trans. Willa and Edwin Muir. New York: Schocken Books.
15. **Kant, Immanuel** (1998). *Critique of Pure Reason.* Trans. Paul Guyer and Allen W. Wood. Cambridge: Cambridge University Press.

16. **Kojeve, Alexandre** (1969). *Introduction to the Reading of Hegel.* Trans. James H. Nichols Jr. Ithaca: Cornell University Press.
17. **Kuhn, Thomas** (1962). *The Structure of Scientific Revolutions.* Chicago: University of Chicago Press.
18. **Leibniz, Gottfried Wilhelm** (1991). *Monadology: An Edition for Students.* Trans. Nicholas Rescher. Pittsburgh: University of Pittsburgh Press.
19. **London, Jack** (1993). *Martin Eden.* New York: Penguin Classics.
20. **Marx, Karl, Engels, Friedrich** (1947). *The German Ideology.* New York: International Publishers.
21. **Nietzsche, Friedrich** (1961). *Thus Spoke Zarathustra.* Trans. R. J. Hollingdale. London: Penguin.
22. **Nietzsche, Friedrich** (2006). *On the Genealogy of Morality.* Trans. Carol Diethe. Cambridge: Cambridge University Press.
23. **Orwell, George** (1950). *Nineteen Eighty-Four.* New York: Signet Classics.
24. **Plato** (1968). *The Republic.* Trans. Allan Bloom. New York: Basic Books.
25. **Popper, Karl** (1945). *The Open Society and Its Enemies.* Princeton: Princeton University Press.
26. **Ricoeur, Paul** (1974). *The Conflict of Interpretations: Essays in Hermeneutics.* Trans. Don Ihde. Evanston: Northwestern University Press.
27. **Russell, Bertrand** (1945). *A History of Western Philosophy.* New York: Simon & Schuster.
28. **Sartre, Jean-Paul** (1992). *Being and Nothingness.* Trans. Hazel Barnes. New York: Washington Square Press.
29. **Schleiermacher, Friedrich** (1977). *Hermeneutics: The Handwritten Manuscripts.* Trans. James Duke and Jack Forstman. Atlanta: Scholars Press.
30. **Shakespeare, William** (2003). *Hamlet.* New York: Simon & Schuster.

31. **Spinoza, Baruch** (1996). *Ethics.* Trans. Edwin Curley. London: Penguin.
32. **Steinbeck, John** (2006). *The Grapes of Wrath.* New York: Penguin.
33. **Tolstoy, Leo** (2000). *Anna Karenina.* Trans. Richard Pevear and Larissa Volokhonsky. New York: Penguin.
34. **Tolstoy, Leo** (2008). *War and Peace.* Trans. Richard Pevear and Larissa Volokhonsky. New York: Vintage.
35. **Wittgenstein, Ludwig** (1922). *Tractatus Logico-Philosophicus.* Trans. C. K. Ogden. London: Routledge.